SILVER TIP SHOES
Never Wear Through
AT THE TOES.
METAL TIPS AFFORD THE ONLY PROTECTION AGAINST WEAR OF TOES OF BOOTS AND SHOES

AMERICAN ADVERTISING POSTERS

OF THE NINETEENTH CENTURY

From the Bella C. Landauer Collection
of The New-York Historical Society

MARY BLACK

DOVER PUBLICATIONS, INC., NEW YORK

Copyright © 1976 by The New-York Historical Society.
All rights reserved under Pan American and International Copyright Conventions.

Published in Canada by General Publishing Company, Ltd., 30 Lesmill Road, Don Mills, Toronto, Ontario.
Published in the United Kingdom by Constable and Company, Ltd., 10 Orange Street, London WC2H 7EG.

American Advertising Posters of the Nineteenth Century from the Bella C. Landauer Collection of The New-York Historical Society is a new work, first published by Dover Publications, Inc., in 1976.

International Standard Book Number: 0-486-23356-1
Library of Congress Catalog Card Number: 76-20834

Manufactured in the United States of America
Dover Publications, Inc.
180 Varick Street
New York, N.Y. 10014

Introduction

When she was in the city on Saturday Bella Landauer frequently followed the old New York custom of spending the afternoon at the theatre or at the movies. Sometimes she went with family members or friends, but often she was alone. That was the case on April 23, 1960, when she attended a matinee at the old Loews Theatre on East 72nd Street at Third Avenue to see Yul Brynner star in the movie *Solomon and Sheba* (his co-star was Gina Lollobrigida). Midway through the performance she was seized with a heart attack and died later that afternoon after being taken by ambulance to her apartment in the Drake Hotel. She was 85 years old, and it was the kind of exit for which she had frequently expressed a preference, dreading any incapacity which might leave her an invalid.

Many weekdays and most Sundays Mrs. Landauer followed another schedule, working or talking shop with a wide circle of acquaintances and friends who visited her in her room at the New-York Historical Society. In the Landauer Room her vast collection of American advertising was assembled in big black boxes and folio-sized brown paper scrapbooks, all carefully numbered on the spine to categorize the eclectic contents within.

Those who knew her best characterized Bella Landauer as a whirlwind. She said of herself, "Some fireworks shoot off in all directions," an attempt to explain her wide-ranging collecting interests, which extended to every kind of advertising, old or new. For almost forty years this remarkable woman's energies were spent in piling up a mountain of material—bookplates, theatre programs, sheet music, posters, billheads, trade cards, catalogs, calendars, matchboxes, labels, tickets and promotional literature and objects.

Early in the search, an acquaintance remarked, "I hear you are only collecting from scrap baskets." At the Landauer house, however, scrap baskets were almost never the source for her collection. There, wine labels were promptly stripped from bottles, programs and tickets were punctiliously hoarded from weekly forays to the theatre, and printed attachments were snipped from dresses and pillows—despite the stern admonition that some were not to be removed, "under penalty of the law." All of these were added to low foothills of purchased, traded and donated advertisements. Later, the accumulations were sorted by subject and transferred to open boxes. Duplicates were reserved for the Harvard Business Library and the Print Department of the Metropolitan Museum; some small special categories were given to the New York Public Library and to the libraries of Dartmouth, Radcliffe and Vassar Colleges. Within four decades of collecting, however, more than a million neatly classified pieces were pasted in the notebooks or assembled in the boxes at the New-York Historical Society.

Mrs. Landauer had an extraordinary sense of cultural history, one that was constantly expanding as she found additional material for individual business houses or made connections between allied or adjacent factories and the lithography or engraving houses which printed their advertisements. She also had the eyes to see and the wit to know that if she preserved *every* advertisement that came her way she might leave decisions of selection to later generations.

Mrs. Landauer's dedicated interest began quietly enough as an occupation for her middle years. Her doctor had ordered her to rest as her health failed after years of energetic volunteer service during the First World War. Her efforts for servicemen through the American Volunteer Field Service were in keeping with her personal motto, "Lend a hand." It took on a wider definition as she collected old and new advertising material, preserving it for the future. The gathering covered every field of American business with a thoroughness that led one graphic designer to use a squirrel as the central device on one of the many bookplates that she commissioned for herself.

Her collecting began with several scrapbooks of bookplates bought—with characteristic kindheartedness—to help a young man in need of money. On a warm summer evening she idly leafed through her new acquisition and an enthusiasm was born for small, fine engravings. Soon she was visiting book and print dealers to locate bookplates to add to her collection. In a July 1959 article in *The New-York Historical Society Quarterly* called "Collecting and Recollecting," Mrs. Landauer wrote apologetically, "My start in life as a collector came through acquiring stolen goods." Shortly after her original purchase, a dealer who knew of her search mentioned a number of bookplates that he had in stock. Mrs. Landauer observed in each case that she already owned an example, and subsequently learned that the young man she helped had departed with her notebooks as he left the shop's employ.

In an effort to learn more about the examples that she assembled, Mrs. Landauer called and wrote to innumerable collectors and experts, a practice that she maintained throughout her long life. Among the most important of the people that she turned to for information about bookplates was William E. Baillie. He enthusiastically shared his knowledge with the new devotee, and Mrs. Landauer was soon adding interesting and valuable items to her collection with the advice and encouragement of Mr. Baillie and his wife.

Branching out in a way that she was frequently to repeat, Mrs. Landauer soon turned to buying merchants' trade cards. These small cards, engraved or lithographed with shopkeepers' and manufacturers' names, addresses and specialties, were frequently enriched with decorative designs, views of shops and factories and pictures of their products. The tiny but precise depictions of clothing, building, plumbing, transportation, cleaning, printing and engraving businesses awakened another interest; Mrs. Landauer began to search for additional material to supplement the information on the trade cards, stimulated and aided in the quest by Charles Tuttle, the Rutland, Vermont, publisher and book dealer.

As she saved and rescued examples of American advertising, Mrs. Landauer marshalled the material into orderly ranks. Today the assembly works almost as a time machine; marching backward from decade to decade, it establishes a picture of American business and industry from mid-twentieth century back to the mid-nineteenth century.

In the process, Mrs. Landauer was retracing the American experience of her own family and that of her husband. Her grandfather, Seymour Dittman, had come from southern Germany in the middle of last century in one of the waves of migration that arrived in increasing volume on these shores—that of the 1850s being of prosperous and well-educated Germans. Her father, Adolph Fackenthal, was a corset manufacturer whose firm was eventually acquired by the forerunner of the contemporary company Lily Of France. Thus, the boned torture chamber that molded the fashionable hourglass figure of the last half of the nineteenth century was her parent's stock in trade. Trade cards and advertisements for corsets, boning, strings, laces and hooks, for cork or down-filled bustles, and for concentric-ringed hoopskirts fill an entire scrapbook volume of the collection.

Her husband, Ian Nathan Landauer, came to America in 1880 from Alsace-Lorraine. With his parents' consent he had fled conscription into the German army by embarking for America. He was only fourteen, and carried with him a letter of introduction from his father to an earlier émigré from the same region, then established in New York as a handkerchief manufacturer. Young Landauer was employed as an office boy. Like many another arrival intent on making his way in the world of the lower East Side, he saved some money by making the store of the import business his headquarters, sleeping on the sales counter at night. By 1895 he had worked his way up to salesman. At the age of 34 he finally felt prosperous enough to ask Bella Clara Fackenthal to marry him. Later she was to tell her two boys that while she had been admired and courted by other young men, she had wanted only to marry Ian Landauer, but that he paid her no notice until he was able to support her adequately.

As a third-generation New Yorker and the daughter of a prosperous manufacturer, Bella had attended Miss Hewitt's classes. There she learned to express herself fluently (and quickly) in both French and English; German was the heritage of her ancestry; over the years she acquired a reading knowledge of Spanish and Italian. Miss Hewitt's was her only formal education, since her father disapproved of college for women, even though he could easily have provided it for his only child.

As a young wife, married to a man nine years her senior, Mrs. Landauer began to read extensively, travel widely and make frequent forays to the opera and theatre. Her interests and her enthusiasms were many, and her informal education continued, channeled and nourished by her energetic personality and exploring mind. Her first child, James, was born in 1902 in her grandmother's house at 108 East 60th Street (a building that still stands). In 1904, Bella and Ian Landauer moved to their own house in a developing section of town at 11 West 74th Street, also standing today. A second son, William, was born in 1906, and until the First World War Mrs. Landauer's energies were spent on home and family.

In 1923, she started to amass her collections; eventually they were to fill an entire floor of the West 74th Street home and extend to the basement. Within three years the available space there could no longer accommodate the rapidly growing archive. When the Drake Hotel on Park Avenue was completed in the early 1930s, the Landauers decided to give up their town house and to move there; by then the entire collection had been transferred to the New-York Historical Society. The Drake was to be Mrs. Landauer's home for the rest of her life.

Every year there were trips to Paris, where she haunted the bookshops and became a member of the Vieux Papiers Society. There were frequent visits to Hanover, New Hampshire, and forays into the surrounding countryside that yielded up many early treasures of Vermont and New Hampshire advertising miscellany. Several articles and slim volumes on her collecting interests were published. These included: *Leaves of Music by Walt Whitman; Trivial Washingtonia; Pre-frigidaire Ice Ephemera;* "Chalking the Hat"; "Striking the Right Note in Advertising"; "Selections from the Music Collection"; and "Business, The New Maecenas."

In New York, Harry Shaw Newman of the Old Print Shop led her to rich sources of advertising material, as did Goodspeed's Book Shop in Boston; the famed book dealer Dr. A. S. W. Rosenbach was also to help her generously in locating books, posters and prints. Both Mr. Baillie and Mr. Tuttle continued to advise her. Bookplates and trade cards were the beginning, but as the years went by, aviation, automobile and sheet-music collections took form. A Walt Disney collection grew alongside a Walt Whitman one (the latter a gift to the New York Public Library); letters and international playbills of her favorite American dramatist, Eugene O'Neill, were assembled and given to the Baker Library in Hanover, New Hampshire.

Her own account of the transfer of the bulk of the collection from her West Side brownstone to its quarters at the New-York Historical Society best describes the move:

> The late Alexander J. Wall, then Director, was originally responsible for my joining the Society in 1926, but he was at a loss where to place me and my collection of bookplates and trade cards, for there was no room available except in an unused kitchen under the eaves of the old building at 170 Central Park West. There I struggled for many years, while guards patiently carried up buckets of hot water, which is essential to my work in soaking off plates or washing prints. There was no telephone in my scant quarters and, except for two exhibitions in the Society's galleries in the spring of 1929 and summer of 1930, no visitor ever examined my collection or saw my pathetic domain. Still, I persevered in enlarging and arranging my treasures and finally emerged to public view when the building sprouted wings in 1939. Since then, countless people have used the resources gathered in my room and many kind friends have contributed to its improvement. On Sunday afternoons I often feel as if their presence still hovers over my room.

Thousands of posters, trade cards, railroad ephemera, tobacco items, war letters and valentines now testify to Mrs. Landauer's perseverance. These are interspersed with construction and hardware advertising, dressmakers' and hatters' notices, and the corset and shoemakers' cards that also interested and pleased her. Some of Mrs. Landauer's titles for the large scrapbooks indicate the range: "Jewelry, Lawyers, Leather Goods . . . Optical, Packing, Paper, Plastics . . . Radium, Real Estate, Religion . . . Undertakers, Warehouses, and Waterworks."

Of the mountain that rose, she wrote modestly and offhandedly:

> Trivia has always fascinated me. My collection continues to branch out almost spontaneously into many fields of interest, all equally fascinating, forming a vivid picture of the business and professional history of America. . . . The goodwill of dealers, who seemed to take personal pride in finding treasures to add to my collection, has been of great aid and I am duly grateful for their assistance. I still marvel that the ephemera which for so many years had been spurned now has finally become important and desirable. . . . "Last autumn's chestnuts, rather passées,/ Are now presented as marrons glacées."

One hundred and one advertising posters have now been

selected as a sampling of the Bella Clara Landauer Collection of American Advertising. They stand as a small illustration of the incomparable resource that Mrs. Landauer labelled Trivia and Ephemera. The selection is related to the New York consumer from 1840 to 1898 and presents an absorbing portrait of the city's streets, social life, homes and offices, entertainment and citizenry.

The posters are the focal point of an exhibition of material from the collection, a major presentation never seen by the public before. Dr. James J. Heslin, director of the Society, first envisioned the show, which is made possible by means of a grant from Mobil Oil Corporation, part of its Bicentennial celebration of the American poster. In assembling, organizing and preparing the materials for exhibition, enthusiastic cooperation and support have been given by the Society's librarian, James Gregory.

All the advertising pieces assembled by Mrs. Landauer have been surveyed for this exhibition. Many have been removed from her black boxes and scrapbooks and assembled in categories closely related to those she originally established. Preparation of the material for publication and display was done by Loren Klingle, Miguel Martinez and Miguel Colon—and, most of all, by Ellen Leslie Schutz of the Museum Department, who typed the manuscript for this book in its several editions, and removed and prepared thousands of advertising items from the scrapbooks assembled by Mrs. Landauer. Mary Alice Kennedy, assistant curator, did the initial record and catalog of the posters.

From Dover Publications, Hayward and Blanche Cirker, publishers, joined editor Stanley Appelbaum in making the selection for this book. James D. Landauer, trustee of the New-York Historical Society, wrote the foreword, provided numerous anecdotes and verified facts concerning his mother. Mr. William C. Wheeler, senior vice-president of Coats & Clark, identified the locale seen in one of the posters; L. K. Goodstal of the Remington Gun Museum in Ilion, New York, assisted with information concerning the Remington house and museum there; Gene K. Baker of the Ferry-Morse Seed Co. supplied data about his firm; Roderick Blackburn, business manager of the Albany Institute of History and Art, helped in documenting two posters of Albany tobacco firms; Oliver O. Jensen, senior editor and vice-president of *American Heritage*, identified a railroad engine. Stanley Appelbaum supplied information about the nineteenth-century theatre in New York. M. J. Gladstone, president of the Publishing Center for Cultural Resources, suggested some new directions for documenting several posters.

New York, Boston, Hartford, Cincinnati and Buffalo directories were consulted for data relating to products and printing, as were numerous town and business histories. Significantly, many of the advertisements and other materials in the Landauer Collection itself provide key information about the poster illustrations. Harry Peter's *America on Stone* (New York, 1931) was helpful in identifying artists, lithographers and engravers, and in estimating the year in which undated posters were published (the Index of Artists, Engravers, Lithographers, Printers and Publishers of the 101 posters may be thought of as a supplement to Peter's useful listings). George C. D. Odell's 15-volume work *Annals of the New York Stage* (New York, 1927–49) was a valuable guide in identifying actors, theatres and plots of plays advertised in the theatrical posters. New York insurance and real-estate maps aided in locating many of the advertisers, while the *Dictionary of American Biography* was frequently consulted for life histories of American businessmen. R. W. G. Vail's history of the New-York Historical Society, *Knickerbocker Birthday* (New York, 1954), provided information on the Egyptian collection now in the Brooklyn Museum.

From Automatodeon (the steam musical instrument mounted on an ornate circus wagon) through Zylobalsamum (the magic ingredient in a hair restorative) these posters are an index to products or services which were once made, used, discarded, observed or sold in New York. A late nineteenth-century newspaper writer, celebrating the invention of the albertype and its use by the Forbes Lithography Manufacturing Company of Boston to reproduce works by Raphael, Titian, Turner and Bonheur, typifies the disdain expressed by many contemporaries in viewing these advertisements avidly collected by nineteenth-century shopkeepers, farmers and housewives:

> They seem to herald the day when the cheap lithographs of Nassau Street and the more wretched premium travesties on good chromo-printing, shall be displaced by real, worthy representations. . . . Such pictures . . . are the levellers-up; they bring the cottage nearer to the home of luxury. . . .

While this *Boston Evening Transcript* writer saw the art poster as a "leveller-up," it is really these practical—often beautiful—examples of advertising that are a clear demonstration of the steps the "cottager" took to reach "the home of luxury." Each image provides valuable insight into the material culture of the last half of the nineteenth century.

Foreword

The Landauer Collection is the result of the devoted and intelligent efforts of a wonderful lady, whose dedication to The New-York Historical Society and the art of collecting is nationally recognized. Year after year she applied her varied talents to the completion and excellence of a compilation of early American advertising. Its use and its enjoyment by the public was the only reward she desired.

You may ask why the writer is so certain of the above facts. The answer is simply that I am one of her two sons.

JAMES D. LANDAUER

A NOTE ON THE PLATES

The chronological sequence of the posters is occasionally interrupted in order to effect more visually pleasing or more meaningful combinations. (For technical reasons all the color plates are grouped together before the black-and-white sequence resumes.) The Chronological Index of Posters at the end of the book indicates their exact ordering in time. The Index of Advertisers and the Index of Artists, Engravers, Lithographers, Printers and Publishers, both alphabetical, contain further information on the addresses of the various firms.

FIRTH, HALL & POND

PIANOFORTE & MUSIC WAREHOUSE

Nº 1 Franklin Square New York.

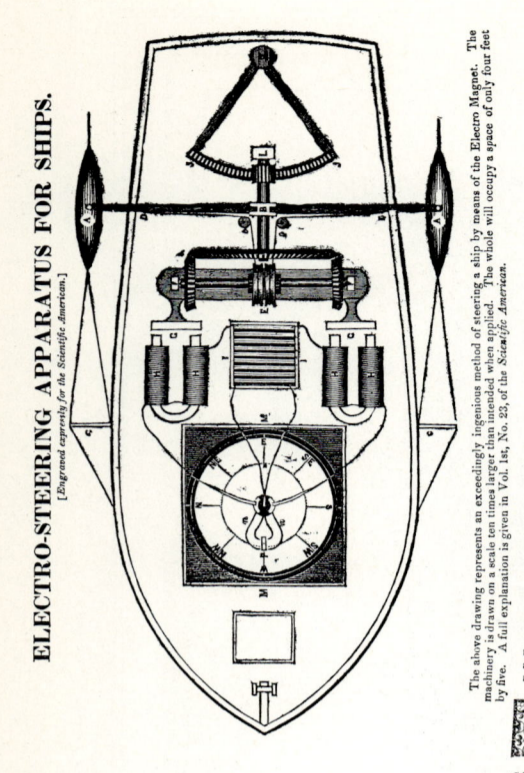

ELECTRO-STEERING APPARATUS FOR SHIPS.
[Engraved expressly for the Scientific American.]

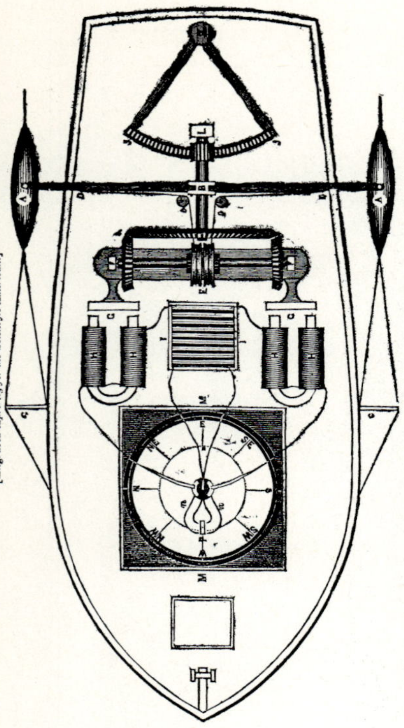

The above drawing represents an exceedingly ingenious method of steering a ship by means of the Electro Magnet. The machinery is drawn on a scale ten times larger than intended when applied. The whole will occupy a space of only four feet by five. A full explanation is given in Vol. 1st, No. 25, of the *Scientific American.*

SHIP TRANSPORTATION ON RAIL-ROADS.
[Engraved expressly for the Scientific American.]

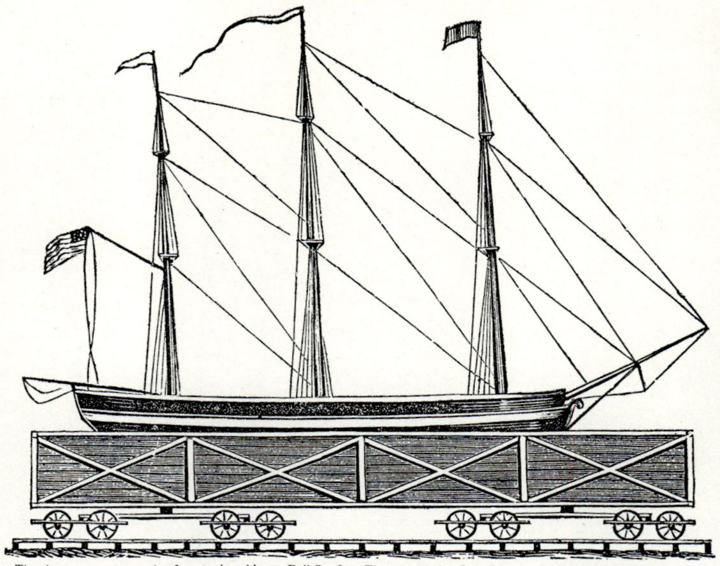

The above represents a plan for carrying ships on Rail-Roads. The vessel being floated into a large box or lock filled with water, the whole is then drawn up on to the track. Should the New-York and Erie Rail-Road be constructed with a firm double track, and a ship car placed thereon, it would not only insure a great amount of ship building on the lakes, but in case of war our Government might readily put on a large naval force. A full explanation may be found in the 15th No. Vol. 1st, of the *Scientific American.*

THE PLUMB AND LEVEL INDICATOR.
[Engraved expressly for the Scientific American.]

Every carpenter, mason, brick-layer and mill-wright will readily appreciate the utility of a more ready method of ascertaining the position of grounds, walls and timbers, than by the use of the spirit level, or plumb line in combination with a bevel and scale. We believe the instrument above represented, is new; at least we have neither seen nor heard of anything of the kind, though we must admit that it is a wonder that something of the kind has not been both invented and brought into general use long before this.

EXPLANATION.—This "indicator" consists of a square frame 8 to 12 inches in diameter, and within which is a circular plate dial divided at its periphery into 360 degrees, and each quadrant of the circle being marked to indicate the degrees from 0 to 90. In the centre of the circle is a delicate axle-pin on which is mounted an index needle, terminating at one end in a metallic ball. This dial-plate may be made of glass that the index may be seen from either side; but it is best to make them of brass or wood, with a glass in front for the preservation of the dial. It will be understood that the proper position of the instrument, is vertical, and that the weight of the ball will keep the index in a perpendicular position; so that either the bottom or the side of the frame being placed against a horizontal line, vertical, or oblique surface, the index will readily indicate whatever variation there may be, from a perpendicular or a horizontal line. The inventor has put in progress measures for securing a patent. *Scientific American,* Vol. 1st, No. 40.

ELECTRO-MAGNETIC ENGINE.
[Engraved expressly for the Scientific American.]

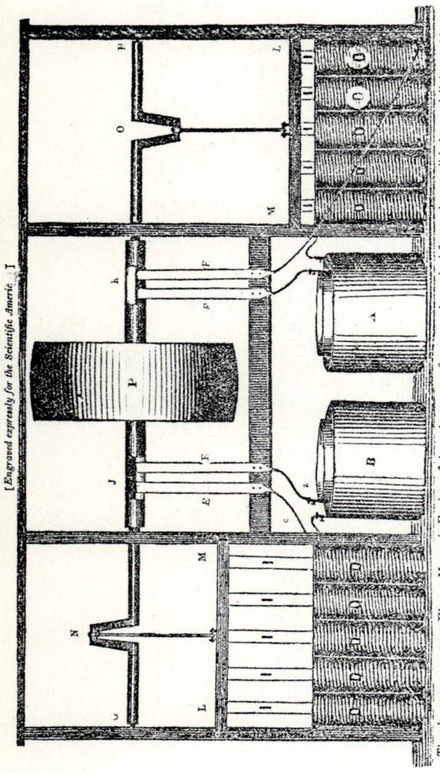

The above represents an Electro-Magnetic Engine, of about the power of one man, just suited for turning small lathes and light machinery. The expense is quite small. Full explanation in *Scientific American,* Vol. 1st, No. 24.

THE NEW-YORK
SCIENTIFIC AMERICAN:
The Advocate of Industry and Enterprise, and Journal of Mechanical and other Improvements.

Published Weekly, at the Sun Building, corner Fulton & Nassau-Sts.

BY MUNN & COMPANY.

RUFUS PORTER, Editor.

☞ EACH NUMBER of this paper is furnished with from

THREE TO SIX ORIGINAL ENGRAVINGS,

Cut every week at a heavy expense, illustrative of

NEW INVENTIONS, SCIENTIFIC PRINCIPLES, AND CURIOUS WORKS,

And contains as much Interesting Intelligence as SIX ORDINARY DAILY PAPERS, consisting of Notices of the PROGRESS OF MECHANICAL and other SCIENTIFIC IMPROVEMENTS,—American and Foreign INVENTIONS,—Catalogues of AMERICAN PATENTS,—SCIENTIFIC ESSAYS, illustrative of the Principles of the Sciences of

MECHANICS, CHEMISTRY & ARCHITECTURE,

INSTRUCTIONS in various ARTS & TRADES,—Curious Philosophical Experiments,—MISCELLANEOUS INTELLIGENCE, Poetry, and Music.

This paper is especially entitled to the patronage of MECHANICS and MANUFACTURERS, being devoted to the interests of those classes; but is particularly useful to FARMERS, as it will not only apprise them of IMPROVEMENTS in AGRICULTURAL IMPLEMENTS, but INSTRUCT them in various MECHANICAL TRADES, and guard them against impositions. As a FAMILY NEWSPAPER, it will convey more USEFUL INTELLIGENCE to children and young people, than five times its cost in school instruction.

TERMS.—The SCIENTIFIC AMERICAN is furnished to subscribers at $2 per annum, ONE DOLLAR IN ADVANCE. Five copies will be sent to one address six months, for Four Dollars in advance.

Any person procuring four or more subscribers, will be entitled to a commission of twenty-five cents each. Persons wishing to subscribe, have only to enclose the amount with name and residence, in a letter directed to

MUNN & COMPANY,
PUBLISHERS OF THE "SCIENTIFIC AMERICAN,"
NEW-YORK CITY.

☞ Letters must, in all cases, be POST PAID.

Strangers visiting New-York, are respectfully invited to call at the Office of the Scientific American, Sun Building, corner Fulton and Nassau Sts. where Models of Inventions, &c. may at all times be seen. The Steam Printing Works of the New-York Sun, one of the greatest curiosities in the city, may also be seen in operation, in the same building.

GEN. SEMPLE'S PRAIRIE STEAM-CAR.
[Engraved expressly for the Scientific American.]

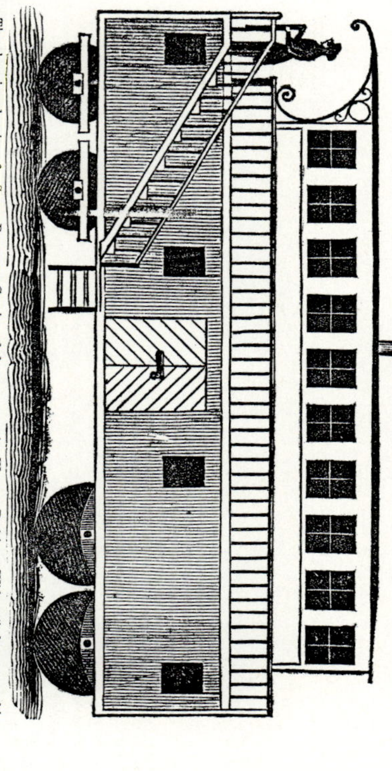

The above is a drawing of a Steam Passenger Car, intended to run over the Western Prairies. Wide cylinders are used in place of the common wheels, in order to prevent sinking into the ground. Full explanation in the *Scientific American,* Vol. 1, No. 26.

THE BULLET ENGINE.
[Engraved expressly for the Scientific American.]

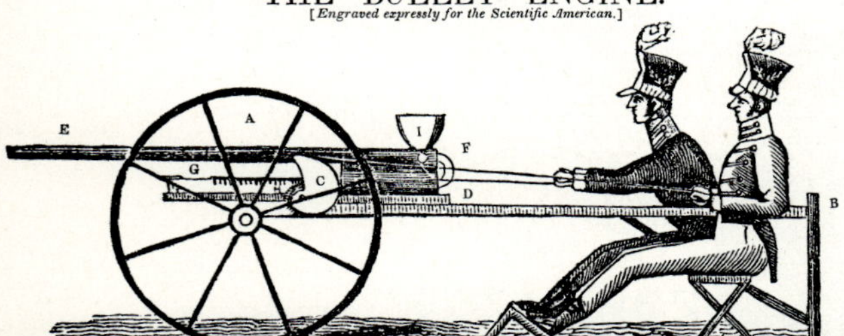

It is an easy thing to prove, that by the aid of a suitable machine, a man of common strength can project four or five bullets with the ordinary force of rifle balls, in less time than he can load and discharge a common musket. The plan introduced above, is for a machine operated upon by two men, for discharging rifle balls. The projecting force is produced by the compression of air. The apparatus is not so heavy but that two men may perform a march with it with ease; and when required to be put into operation, the delay of preparation will not exceed one minute. The discharges may be about thirty per minute. A complete explanation is given in Vol. 1st, No. 36, of the *Scientific American.*

THE ROTARY PLOUGH.
[Engraved expressly for the Scientific American.]

The wheels, or ploughs, of the above, are made of iron plate, convex on one side and concave on the other, similar to a watch crystal. The machine is not drawn at right angles with the direction of the horse, but obliquely. The cost of a machine is about $25. A working model may be seen at the Office of the *Scientific American.* Full explanation in No. 31, Vol. 1st.

SAMUEL C. JOLLIE & CO.

WHOLESALE & RETAIL

Piano Forte, Flute & Music Store,

No. 385 BROADWAY, near White-street, N. Y.

WHERE MAY BE HAD AN ELEGANT ASSORTMENT OF

MUSIC,

FOR THE PIANO FORTE, FLUTE, GUITAR, OR VIOLIN.

ALL THE NEW MUSIC RECEIVED AS SOON AS PUBLISHED.

Manufacturer of Superior Toned Flutes,

With from one to eight keys; also, FLAGEOLETS, CLARIONETS and FIFES, and an elegant assortment of FRENCH and GERMAN GUITARS, with plain and patent heads, of the latest pattern, ACCORDEONS, VIOLINS, VIOLINCELLOS, BOWS and HAIR, VIOLIN PEGS, ROSIN, TUNING FORKS and HAMMERS, and STRINGS for every Instrument.

MUSICAL INSTRUMENTS TUNED & REPAIRED.

N. B.—MUSIC BOUND in a Superior Style, and Music sent to any part of the City.

PROFESSIONAL & VISITING CARDS

Engraved and Printed with the utmost neatness

PAYN & McNAUGHTON,

SIGN OF SEVEN HEADS, NEXT E. CORNING & CO.'S, No. 7 BROADWAY,

ALBANY, N. Y.

PAYN and McNAUGHTON, MANUFACTURERS of TOBACCO, SNUFF, CIGARS, CHOCOLATE AND Prepared Cocoa. Dealers in PIPES, MATCHES, MUSTARD, PLUG TOBACCO AND Imported Cigars, Snuff Boxes &c. No. 7 Broadway, ALBANY, N.Y.

P. & McN. having received the Highest Premium from the New-York State Agricultural Society, as Manufacturers of the best articles above named, beg leave to assure the public, that their

TOBACCO, SNUFF, CIGARS, CHOCOLATE & COCOA,

bearing the accompanying Stamps, are in no way inferior to that submitted to the Agricultural Society, but confidently believe it to be

SUPERIOR TO THAT MANUFACTURED ELSEWHERE.

We Use Rogers' Patent Tobacco Cutting Engine.

Sold Here

PAYN & McNAUGHTON'S PURE GROUND CHOCOLATE, No. 7 BROADWAY, ALBANY, N. Y.

DIRECTIONS.—To one small square (scraped fine), add a pint of milk (heat the same), then fill up with hot water, o suit the taste (say two quarts), which will make a delicious drink (so say all those that have used).

Border labels:

- PAYN & McNAUGHTON'S Fine Smoking Tobacco, Albany.
- PAYN AND McNAUGHTON'S Extra Fine Cut JAMES RIVER CAVENDISH, Albany, N.Y.
- PAYN & McNAUGHTON, Manufacturers of CHOCOLATE, AND PREPARED COCOA. No. 7 Broadway, ALBANY.
- PAYN AND McNAUGHTON'S FINE YELLOW BANK KENTUCKY CHEWING TOBACCO
- Directions for Using PAYN & McNAUGHTON'S PREPARED COCOA. Boil a half tea-cup full in three quarts milk and water (more milk the better,) for fifteen minutes, let it settle, and it is fit for use.
- PAYN AND McNAUGHTON'S ROSE SCENTED MACCOBOY.

NEW LINE BETWEEN
ALBANY & NEWBURG

LANDING AT

Hamburgh, Marlborough, Milton, Poughkeepsie, Hyde Park, Kingston, Rhinebeck, Barrytown, Redhook, Bristol, Westcamp Catskill, Hudson, Coxsackie, Stuyvesant, Baltimore & Coeymans.

On and after MONDAY, October 15th,

The Superior Low Pressure Steame

ST. NICHOLAS

CAPTAIN WILSON,

Will run as a Passage and Freight Boat between Newburgh and Albany, leaving Newburgh

MONDAYS, WEDNESDAYS & FRIDAYS

AT SEVEN O'CLOCK A.M.,

And ALBANY on Tuesdays, Thursdays & Saturdays, at half-past 9 o'clock A.M.

Albany, Oct. 9th, 1849.

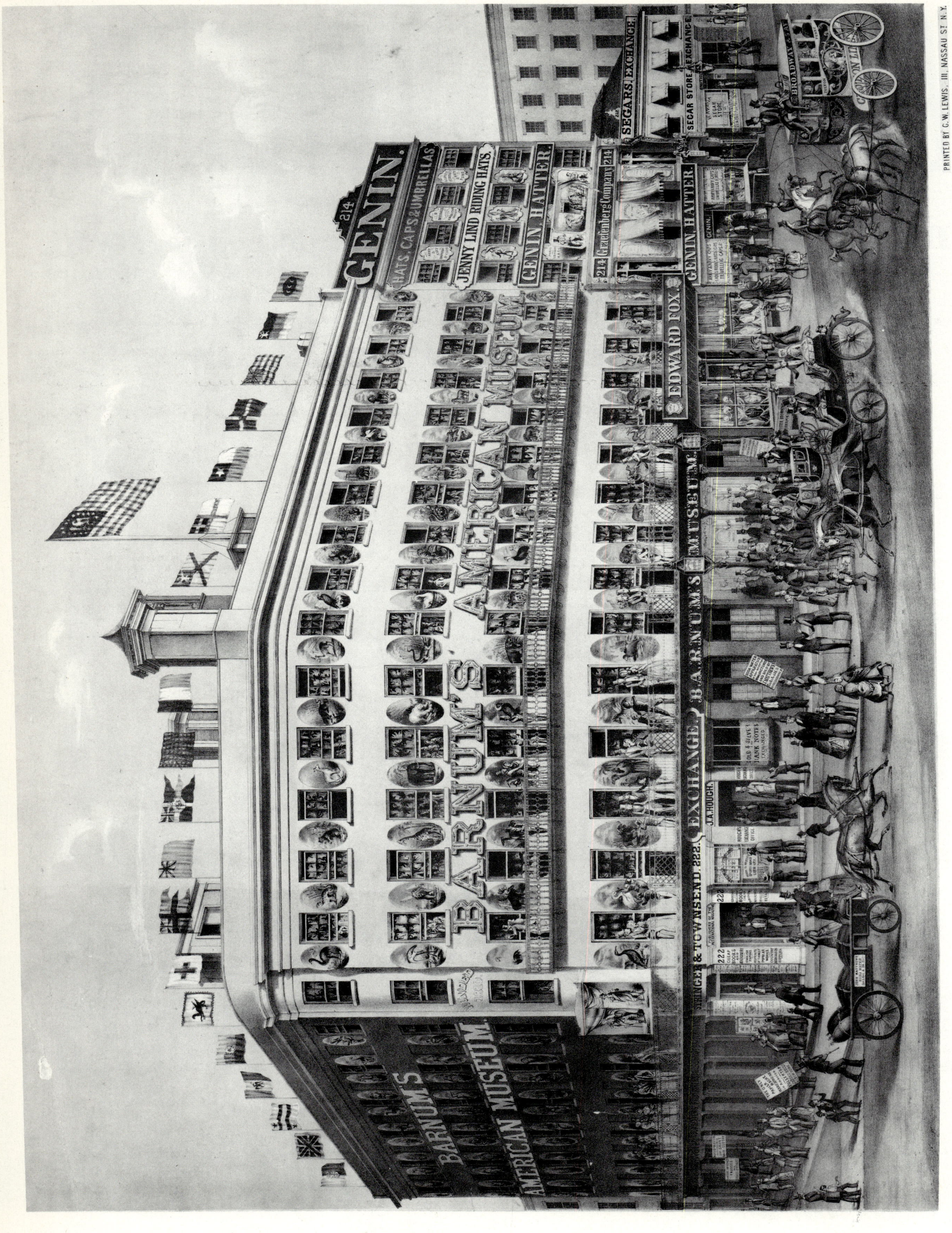

BROWN & SEVERIN, DEL & LITH. 142 FULTON ST. N.Y.

PRINTED BY C.W. LEWIS, 111, NASSAU ST. N.Y.

THE AUTOMATODEON,

OR MUSICAL INSTRUMENT

AS IT APPEARED PASSING CASTLE GARDEN AND THE BATTERY N.Y. APRIL 2ND 1850, DRAWN BY EIGHT SYRIAN CAMELS, AND THE ASIATIC ELEPHANT BOLIVAR, DRIVEN IN THE PROCESSION OF

G. C. QUICK & CO'S MAMMOTH MENAGERIE.

Will Exhibit at   *on*   1850.

JOS. LAING & Co.
LITHOGRAPHERS
EDWARD EVANS
66
68
JOS. LAING & Co.
ENGRAVERS & PRINTERS.
CLOTHING WAREHOUSE.
JOSEPH LAING & Co.
LITHOGRAPHERS,
ENGRAVERS AND PRINTERS,
Bank Notes Cheques, Bills of Exchange, Bills of Lading, Bill Heads, Circulars, CARDS &c.
66
Maps, Plans, Facsimilies, Title Pages, Illuminated Show Cards, Book Covers, LABELS, &c.
FULTON STREET,
NEW-YORK.
WASHINGTON MONUMENT
EDWARD EVANS,
WHOLESALE & RETAIL
CLOTHING WAREHOUSE;
Gents Furnishing Goods of every Description.
66 & 68
Cloths Cassimeres & Vestings of the latest Importations always on hand.
FULTON STREET,
NEW-YORK.

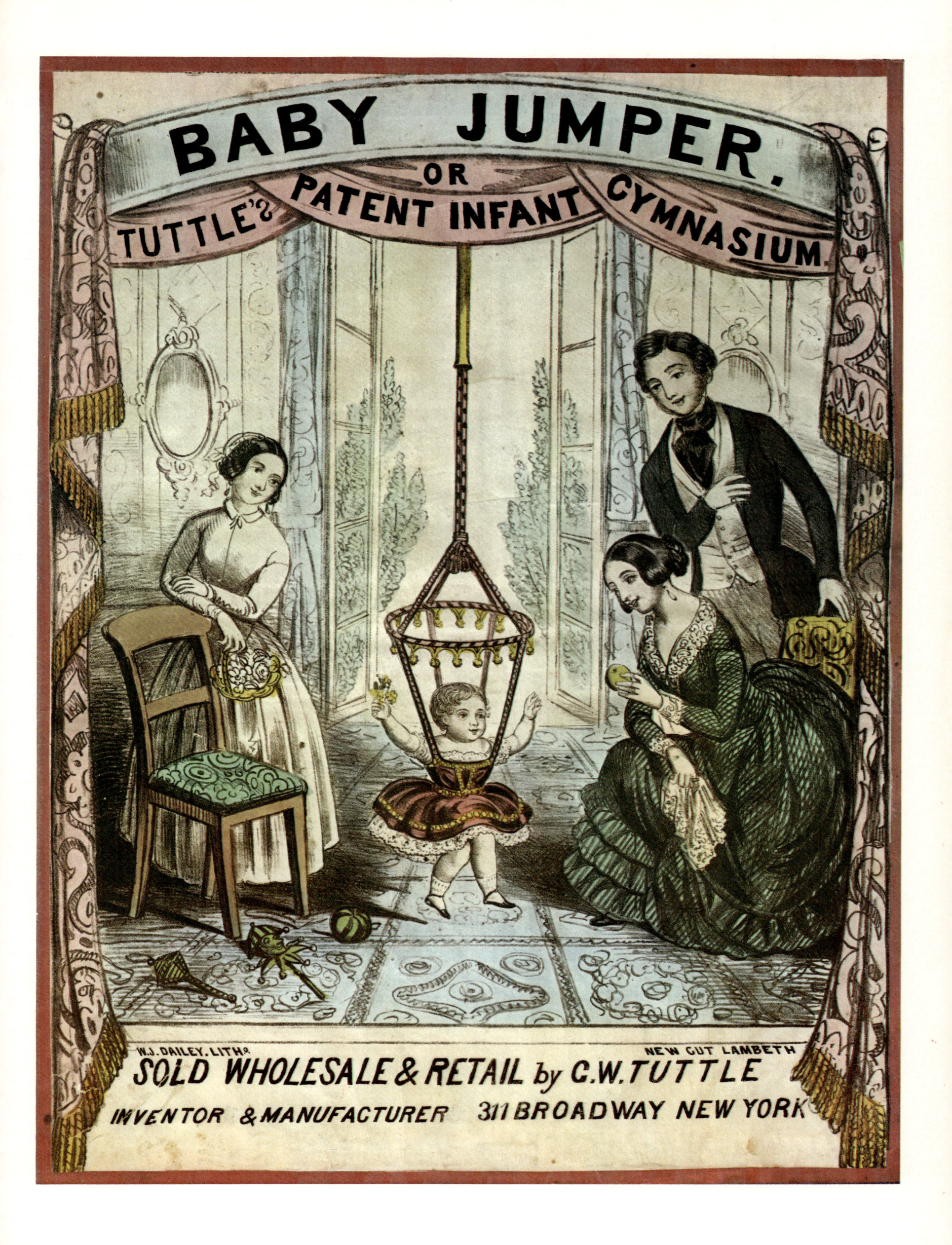

BABY JUMPER.
OR TUTTLE'S PATENT INFANT GYMNASIUM.

W.J. DAILEY, LITH.   NEW CUT LAMBETH

SOLD WHOLESALE & RETAIL by C.W. TUTTLE

INVENTOR & MANUFACTURER   311 BROADWAY NEW YORK

CONGRESS

Stove Polish.

Mrs. S. A. ALLEN'S

Mrs. S.A. ALLEN'S WORLD'S HAIR RESTORER.

FOR THE OLD & THE YOUNG.
IT IS NOT A DYE.

The Only Hair Restorer. The Only Hair Dressing.

Mrs. S.A. ALLEN'S WORLD'S HAIR DRESSING or Zylobalsamum.

FOR THE BALD & THE GREY.

WORLD'S HAIR RESTORER. WORLD'S HAIR DRESSING.

SARONY, MAJOR & KNAPP. LITH., 449 BROADWAY, N.Y.

HENRY MILLER'S
TOBACCO.
HENRY MILLER'S GORGEOUS TOBACCO CHARIOT
AS SEEN IN BROADWAY OPPOSITE ST NICHOLAS HOTEL:
SALES ROOM 116 MAIDEN LANE.
NEW YORK.
LITH. & PRINTED IN TINTS BY SARONY & MAJOR, 117 FULTON ST N.YORK.

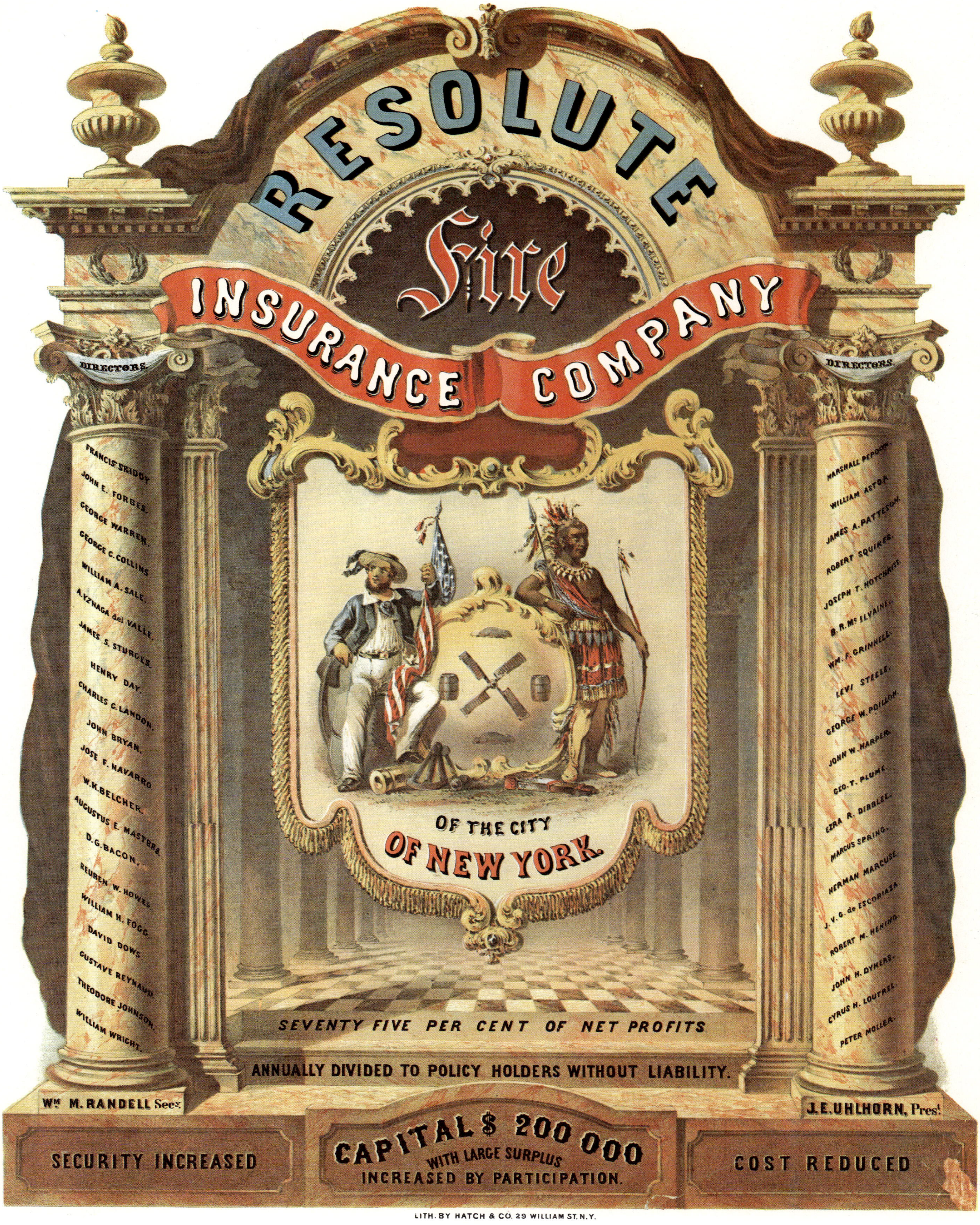

LITH. BY HATCH & CO. 29 WILLIAM ST. N.Y.

LOVE
TOBACCO.
MANUFACTURED BY
MYERS BRO'S AND CO.
RICHMOND, VA.
THE CALVERT LITH. CO. DETROIT, MICH.

NIAGARA LEAP BY THE WONDERFUL BUISLAY FAMILY.

PATENT CYLINDER LITHOGRAPHIC PRINTING MACHINE

R. HOE & CO.,

Manufacturers of

PRINTING MACHINE & SAW

Nos. 29 & 31 GOLD STREET

AND ON

Broome, Sheriff, Columbia and Grand Sts.

NEW YORK.

LONDON, ENG.

1845. - WASON - 1872.
CAR MANUFACTURING. CO.
WASON MANF'G CO. RAILWAY CAR BUILDERS.

E. BUTTERICK & CO'S QUARTERLY REPORT OF NEW YORK FASHIONS,

FOR FALL 1866.

PRINCIPAL OFFICE, 555 BROADWAY, NEW-YORK.

19

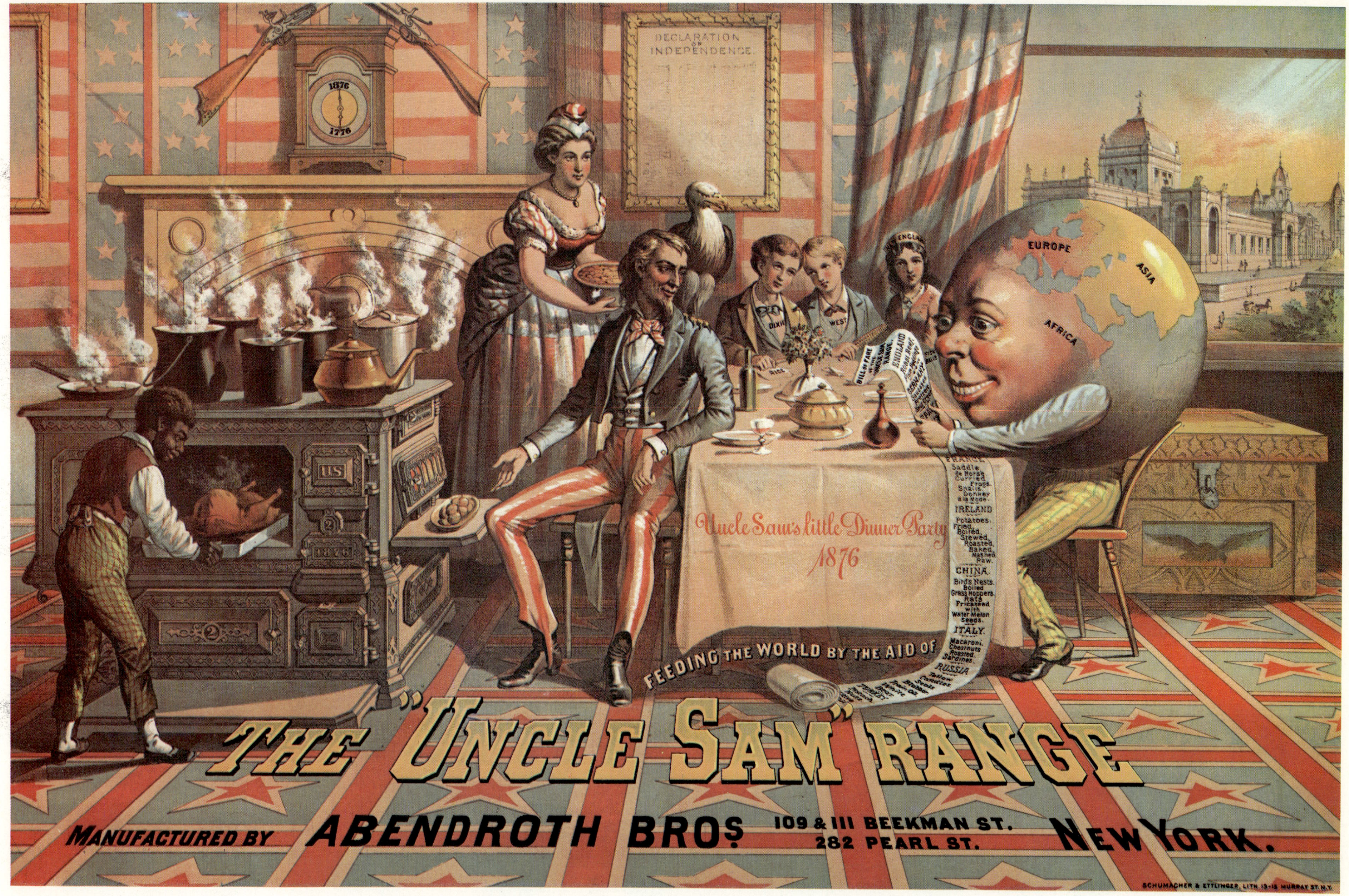
DECLARATION OF INDEPENDENCE
1876
1776
EUROPE
ASIA
AFRICA
DIXIE
WEST
Uncle Sam's little Dinner Party
1876
FRANCE
Saddle de Horse Curried
Frogs
Snails
Donkey a la Mode
IRELAND
Potatoes Fried, Boiled, Stewed, Roasted, Baked, Mashed, Raw.
CHINA
Birds Nests Boiled
Grass Hoppers
Rats Fricaseed with Water Melon Seeds.
ITALY
Macaroni
Chestnuts Roasted
Sardines
RUSSIA
FEEDING THE WORLD BY THE AID OF
THE "UNCLE SAM" RANGE
MANUFACTURED BY ABENDROTH BROS. 109 & 111 BEEKMAN ST. 282 PEARL ST. NEW YORK.
SCHUMACHER & ETTLINGER, LITH 13-15 MURRAY ST. N.Y.

"COLONEL KANE'S COACH."

Published by **J. B. BREWSTER & CO.** OF **25TH STREET**, New York.

CARRIAGE BUILDERS.

MULFORD, CARY & CONKLIN,
Leather and Findings,
NEW YORK.
SWAMP ROBIN
NEW YORK TOWER
THE GREAT EAST RIVER SUSPENSION BRIDGE.
CONNECTING THE CITIES OF NEW YORK & BROOKLYN - FROM NEW YORK LOOKING SOUTH-EAST.
THE BRIDGE APPROACH ON THE NEW YORK SIDE IS OPPOSITE THE CITY HALL, AND THREE MINUTES WALK FROM THE STORE OF
MULFORD, CARY & CONKLIN,
WHOLESALE DEALERS IN LEATHER AND FINDINGS, CALF SKINS, SHEEP SKINS, MOROCCOS,
SHOE MANUFACTURERS GOODS. 34 SPRUCE ST. NEW YORK.
The Bridge crosses the river by a single span of 1.595 ft., suspended by four cables 15½ ins. in diameter, each cable consists of 5.434 parallel steel wires; ultimate strength of each cable, 11,200 tons. The approach on the New York side is 2.492½ ft., approach on the Brooklyn side 1.901 ft., total length, 5.989 ft. Size of towers at high water line, 140×59 ft.
Total height of Towers 277 ft., from high water to roadway 120 ft., from high water to centre of span 135 ft., from roadway to top 158 ft., width of Bridge 85 ft., with tracks for steam cars, roadway for carriages, and walks for foot passengers, and an elevated promenade commanding a view of extraordinary beauty and extent. Estimated total cost, $15.000.000.

The only Route *via* NIAGARA FALLS & SUSPENSION BRIDGE

HAVERLY'S THEATRE!
M. B. CURTIS
SAM'L. PLASTRICK
POSEN.
SAM'L OF POSEN
THE
COMMERCIAL DRUMMER.
STROBRIDGE LITH. CO. CIN & N.Y.
COMMENCING
MONDAY, DEC. 4

THE ORIGINAL
BLACK CROOK
STALACTA
THE STROBRIDGE LITH. CO CIN'TI

D. M. FERRY & CO'S.

CELEBRATED

D.M.F. & CO'S. PREMIUM CABBAGE

D.M.F. & CO'S PURPLE TOP STRAP LEAVED TURNIP

D.M.F. & CO'S IMPROVED YELLOW SWEDE OR RUTA BAGA.

SEEDS

FOR SALE HERE.

THE CALVERT LITH. CO. DETROIT, MICH.

D. M. FERRY & Co's
STANDARD
SEEDS
ARE ALWAYS
GOOD.
NONE. BETTER.
NEW
SEEDS
FOR SALE HERE.

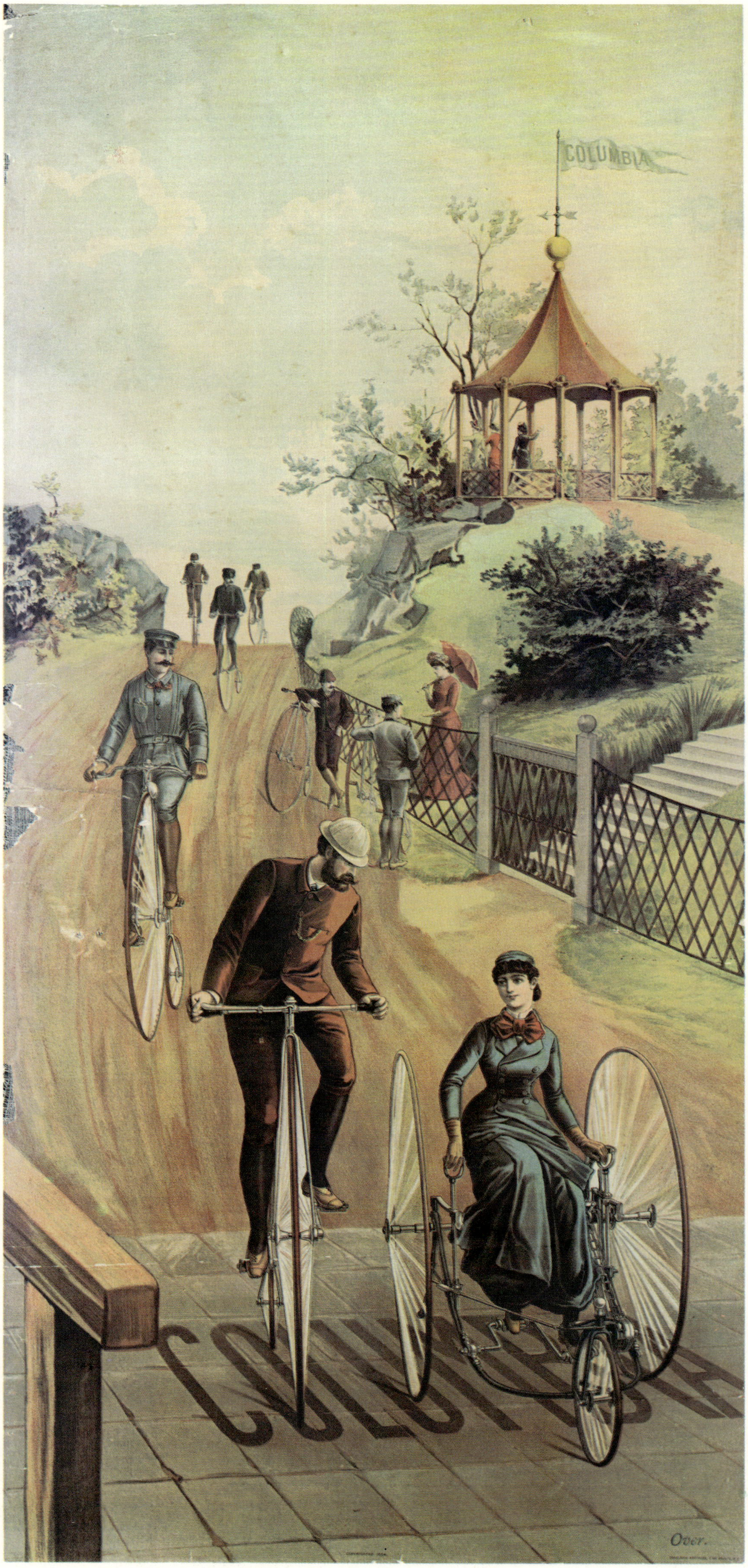
COLUMBIA
Over.

COLUMBIA BICYCLE
1 Mile IN 2 MINUTES 43 SECONDS BY JOHN KEEN
363 Miles IN 26 CONSECUTIVE HOURS BY C. TERRONT AT AGRICULTURAL HALL
1404 MILES IN 6 DAYS BY C. WALLER
205 MILES IN 22 Hours TURNPIKE ROAD BY E. COSTEN AND E. SMYTHE.
AN EVER SADDLED HORSE WHICH EATS NOTHING
212 MILES IN 22 Hours 55 Min. ON THE ROAD FROM London TO BATH and return BY W.S. BRITTEN
1/4 MILE IN 35 5/8 SEC. Chestnut Hill Boston BY G.T. FRANCIS
10 MILES IN 7 HOURS 18 MIN. From BATH To LONDON BY F.E. APPLEYARD
597 WASHINGTON ST.
SEND 3 CENT STAMP FOR CATALOGUE & PRICE LIST CONTAINING FULL INFORMATION TO
THE POPE MFG. CO.
BOSTON MASS.
FORBES CO. BOSTON.

DESCRIPTIVE MUSIC

"THE LAST DAYS OF POMPEII."

TO BE PRODUCED IN FIREWORKS, SEASON OF 1885, UNDER THE DIRECTION OF **JAMES PAIN**, of London,

MANHATTAN BEACH.

GILMORE'S BAND

CHAS. L. DAVIS' CELEBRATED ALVIN JOSLIN COMEDY COMPANY.

180 LAUGHS IN 180 MINUTES.

32

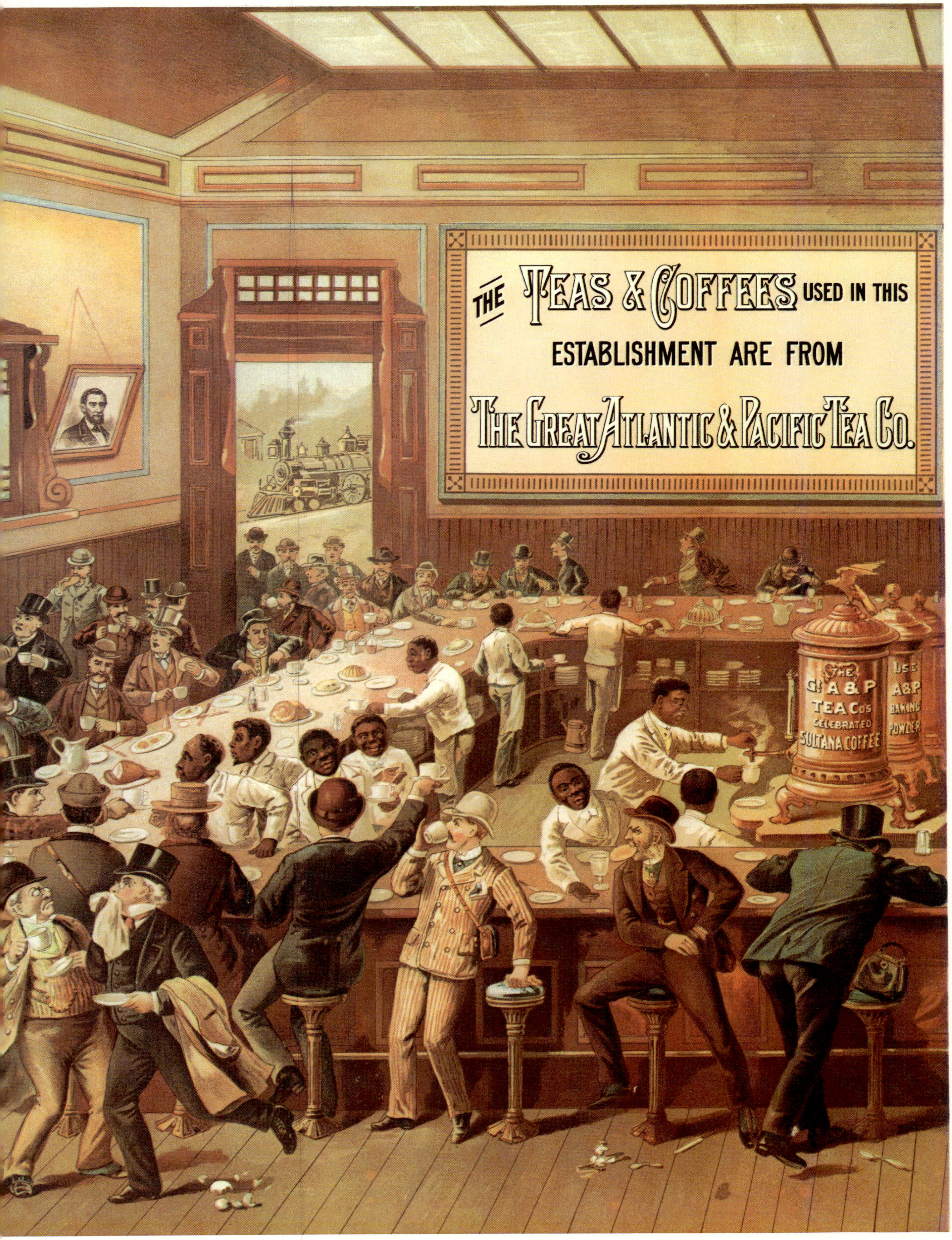

THE TEAS & COFFEES USED IN THIS
ESTABLISHMENT ARE FROM
THE GREAT ATLANTIC & PACIFIC TEA CO.
THE Gt A & P TEA Co's CELEBRATED SULTANA COFFEE
USE A&P BAKING POWDER

INTERIOR VIEW OF MAIN SALESROOM.

HILL BROTHERS, MILLINERY GOODS, 564 & 566 BROADWAY, NEW YORK.

THE J. M. BRUNSWICK & BALKE CO.
NEW YORK. CINCINNATI. CHICAGO. ST. LOUIS & SAN FRANCISCO.
KURZ & ALLISON, LITHO. CHICAGO.

HALSTEAD & Co.
BEEF & PORK PACKERS, LARD REFINERS &c.
194 to 202 FORSYTH ST.
New York
U.S.A.
BEEF & PORK IN PACKAGES SUITABLE FOR FOREIGN & DOMESTIC MARKETS.
MT. VERNON BRAND OF HAMS, LARD, BACON, SHOULDERS & TONGUES.
NIHIL SINE SALE.
Trade Mark.
TRADE MARK.
ESTABLISHED 1844
HALSTEAD & CO. PROVISIONS.
OFFICE
H. BENCKE, LITH. N.Y.

The Remington Fire Engine,
Howe's Patents.
Manufactured by the
REMINGTON AGRICULTURAL Co.
ILION, N.Y.

The "Hoffman House" Bouquet Cigar
FOSTER-HILSON COMPANY
MAKERS.
THE HOFFMAN HOUSE BOUQUET CIGAR
Hon. DAVID B. HILL.
BILLY EDWARDS. Hon. WM. F. CODY, "Buffalo Bill."
Hon. THOMAS W. PALMER, Pres. World's Columbian Exposition.
Hon. GROVER CLEVELAND. Hon. CHAUNCEY M. DEPEW.
GEN. J. M. SCHOFIELD, U. S. A.
TONY PASTOR.
Mr. M. HILSON.
DETECTIVE JACOBS.
PROFESSOR HERRMAN.
NAT. GOODWIN.
VIEW OF THE HOFFMAN HOUSE CORRIDOR

39

40

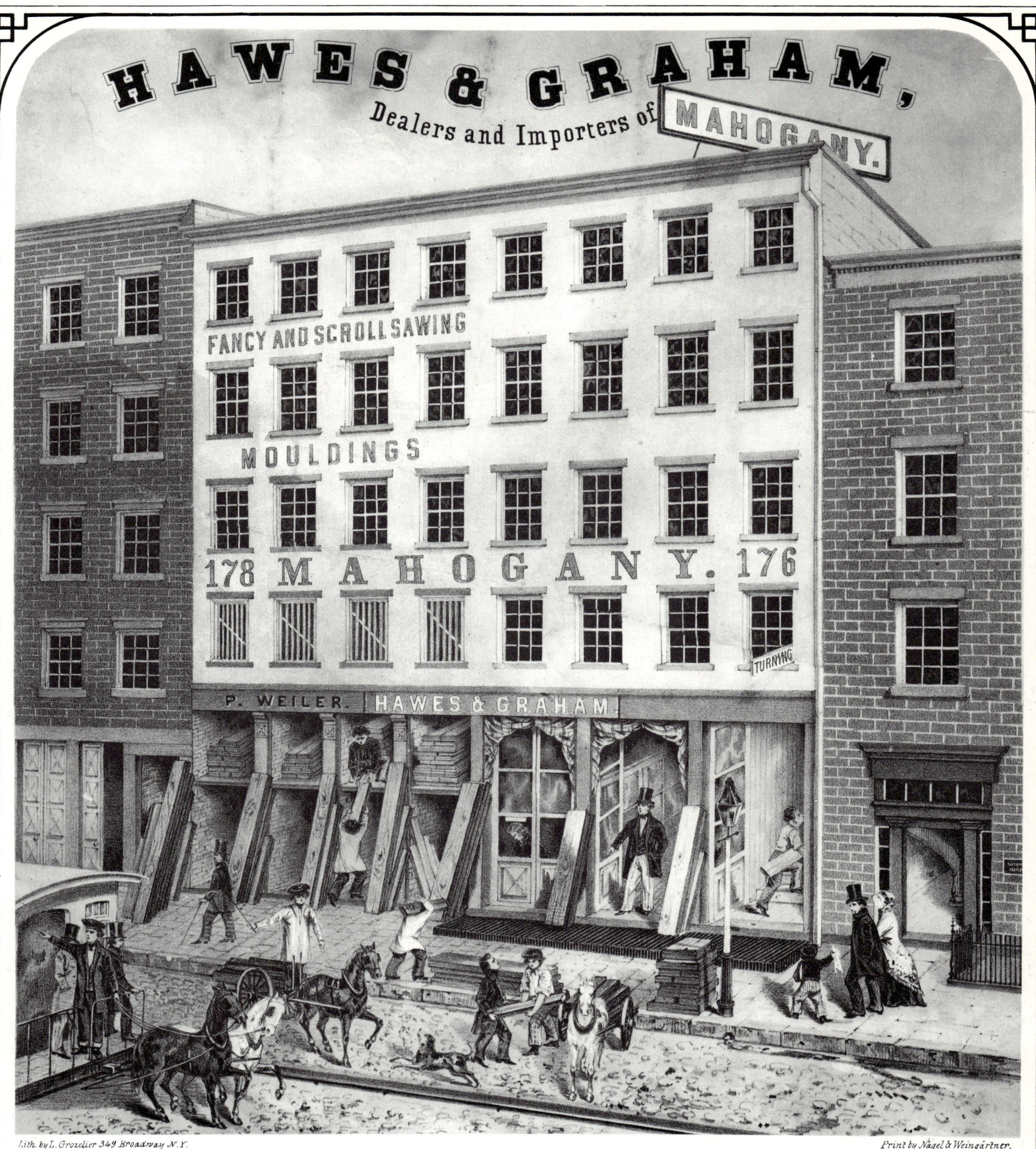

HAWES & GRAHAM,
Dealers and Importers of MAHOGANY.

FANCY AND SCROLL SAWING

MOULDINGS

178 MAHOGANY. 176

TURNING

P. WEILER.   HAWES & GRAHAM.

Lith. by L. Grozelier 349 Broadway N.Y.   Print by Nagel & Weingärtner.

MAHOGANY & ROSE WOOD
176 CENTRE St. 178
NEW YORK

THEIR STOCK embraces the most extensive variety of finely Figured Woods to be found in the United States, viz:—

MAHOGANY, Rose Wood_Satin_Zebra_Ebony_Oak_Spanish & Red Cedar_White Holly_Walnut_Maple & Spruce_ consisting of LOGS, BOARDS, PLANKS & VENEERS.

FRESH OYSTERS!

BY WESTOVERS'
AMBOY LINE.

Through by Express on the
NEW YORK & ERIE RAILROAD.

For Sale Here,

And by the Proprietors, in all the Principal Towns on the New York & Erie Railroad, and also on the *Chenango Valley*, from *Binghamton* to *Utica*.

Customers dealing with this Line shall be sup-plied regularly, according to order, through the season, with the best of AMBOY OYSTERS, at the lowest possible prices.

Sept. 10, 1853.   **C. & R. WESTOVER.**

[From Fairmans' Job Printing Office, Elmira.]

PURIFY THE BLOOD!

MOFFAT'S VEGETABLE LIFE PILLS AND PHŒNIX BITTERS.

The high and envied celebrity which these pre-eminent Medicines have acquired for their invariable efficacy in all the diseases which they profess to cure, has rendered the usual practice of puffing not only unnecessary, but unworthy of them. They are known by their fruits; their good works testify for them, and they thrive not by the faith of the credulous.

IN ALL CASES OF

Asthma.
Acute and Chronic Rheumatism.
Affections of the Bladder and Kidneys.
BILIOUS FEVERS and LIVER COMPLAINTS.
In the south and west, where these diseases prevail they will be found invaluable. Planters, Farmers, and others, who once use these Medicines will never afterwards be without them.
Bilious Cholic.
Serous Looseness.
Biles.   Costiveness.
Colds and Coughs.   Cholic.
CONSUMPTION. Used with the greatest success in this disease.
Corrupt Humors.   Dropsies.

DYSPEPSIA. No person with this distressing disease should delay using these medicines immediately.
Eruptions of the Skin.
Erysipelas.   Flatulency.
FEVER AND AGUE.
For this scourge of the western country these medicines will be found a safe, speedy, and certain remedy. Other medicines leave the system subject to a return of the disease--a cure by these medicines is permanent. Try them, be satisfied, and be cured.
Foulness of the Complexion.
GENERAL DEBILITY.
Gout.   Giddiness.   Gravel.
Headaches, of every kind.

Inward Fever.
Inflammatory Rheumatism.
Impure Blood.   Jaundice.
Loss of Appetite.   Leprosy.
LIVER COMPLAINTS.
MERCURIAL DISEASES.
Never fails to eradicate entirely all the effects of Mercury infinitely sooner than the most powerful preparation of Sarsaparilla.
Night Sweats.   Nervous Debility.
Nervous Complaints, of all kinds.
Organic Affections.
Palpitation of the heart.
Painter's Cholic.
PILES.--The original proprietor of these medicines was cured of piles of 35 years standing by the use of the Life Medicines alone.

Pains in the head, side, back, limbs, joints, and organs.
RHEUMATISM.--Those afflicted with this terrible disease will be sure of relief by the Life Medicines.
Rush of Blood to the head.
Scurvy.
Swellings.
Salt Rheum.
SCROFULA or KING'S EVIL, in its worst forms.
Ulcers of every description.
WORMS of all kinds, are effectually expelled by these medicines. Parents will do well to administer them whenever their existence is suspected. Relief will be certain.

The Life Pills and Phœnix Bitters
PURIFY THE BLOOD,
AND THUS REMOVE ALL DISEASE FROM THE SYSTEM.

A single trial will place the LIFE PILLS and PHŒNIX BITTERS beyond the reach of competition, in the estimation of every patient.

Dr. William B. Moffat's Office,
335 BROADWAY, CORNER OF ANTHONY STREET, N. Y.

The genuine of these medicines are now put up in white wrappers and labels, together with a pamphlet called "Moffat's Good Samaritan," containing the directions, ect., on which is a drawing of Broadway from Wall street to our Office, by which strangers visiting the city can very easily find us. The wrappers and Samaritans are copyrighted, therefore those who procure them with the white wrappers can be assured that they are genuine. Be careful, and do not buy those with yellow wrappers, but if you do, be satisfied that they come direct from us, or don't touch them.

Dr. JOHN WESLEY KELLEY'S DIAMOND PECTORAL.

See Miniature Treatise to be had free of all Agents

Mother is Saved!

Principal Office 259 Bowery N.Y.

A Sure, pleasant and Safe Remedy for all Diseases of the Throat and Chest.

For Sale Here

Price 25 cts. per box or five boxes for $1

Entered, According to Act of Congress, in the year 1852 by Dr. J. W. Kelley, in the Clerk's Office of the District Court of the Southern District of N.Y.

THOMPSON'S
FOLDING LIFE PRESERVING SEAT
PATENTED
in the United States, Great Britain and the Continent of Europe.

GRIFFIN AND CHRISTY'S MINSTRELS

2 & 4 West 24th St., 2 & 4
Adjoining Fifth Ave. Hotel.

G. W. H. Griffin..........Manager | T. Condron......Proprietor

THE FAMILY RESORT

Tuesday Evening, May 28, 1867,
AND DURING THE WEEK.

THE JAPANESE JUGGLERS
In their **AERIAL TRIPS, TOP SPINNING, SLIDING on SHARP SWORDS**, and hundreds of other Native Amusements.

TOO LATE FOR THE TRAIN!   COLUMBIA POLKA!
MOCKING BIRD!   STATUE LOVER,

And other New Acts, constituting the **BEST PERFORMANCE** in the Country.

PROGRAMME.
PART FIRST.—Conversation and Music.

Overture, Reminiscences of Dixie	Griffin and Christy's Minstrels
Chorus Hark Again	Company
I'm as happy as the day is long	Mr. C. Henry
Cat in the Corner	Mr. J. T. Boyce
Sweet Thoughts of Thee	Mr. Geo. Leslie
Why don't They do so now?	Mr. Geo. Christy
Down by the River Side	Mr. C. F. Shattuck
Finale—Conflagration	Company

PART SECOND.—Mirth and Music.

CLOG DANCE, in Original Costume,
Hughes and Hogan.

Ballad, "Selected,"..........................Geo. Leslie

Columbia Polka,
Geo. Christy, Fred. Abbott and J. Hogan.

TOO LATE FOR THE TRAIN!
Burbank, Boyce, Hughes and Hodgkin.

Mocking Bird.......by the wonderful.......Harry Styles

HITS AT THE TIMES, (original,)
Otto Burbank.

Comic Song..........................J. T. Boyce

JAPANESE JUGGLERS
By the Troupe.

PART THIRD.—ORCHESTRAL SELECTIONS.

PART FOURTH—Concluding with THE

STATUE LOVER!

Jake	Geo. Christy	Pete	J. T. Boyce
Old Squintum	G. W. H. Griffin	Mrs. Squintum	W. Hodgkin
Mr. Pugarlic			O. Burbank
Rose			Fred. Abbott

PRICES:
Admission..........................50 Cents
Reserved Orchestra Chairs..........................75 Cents
Family Circle..........................35 Cents

Doors open at Seven.   To commence at Eight o'Clock precisely.

GRAND MATINEE
EVERY SATURDAY, AT 2½ O'CLOCK,
for the accommodation of Ladies and Children,

Admission to Matinee..........................50 Cents
Children to all parts of House..........................25 Cents

BOX OFFICE OPEN FROM 10 A. M. T 5 P. M.

Herald Job Print, corner of Fulton and Nassau Streets.

BARNUM'S AMERICAN MUSEUM
Cor. Broadway and Ann St., opposite St. Paul's Church.

Admittance to the whole Museum, the Picture Gallery, the Natural History Department, the Happy Family, and the Cosmorama Room, as well as the Entertainments in the Lecture Room..25 Cents Children under 10 years..........12 1-2 Cents. Seats in the Parquet and First Balcony..One Shilling extra
MORNING VISITORS ADMITTED TO THE AFTERNOON PERFORMANCES FREE.

Gen'l Tom Thumb
as TOM TIT

In the New Moral Drama of **DRED**, now being performed **EVERY EVENING**, and **WEDNESDAY** and **SATURDAY AFTERNOONS**, to crowded and delighted audiences.

LARGEST SNAKES
IN THE WORLD.

The Newburyport, Mass. Herald says: "The brig Planet, just arrived from Africa, brought to Salem several Monster Snakes Anacondas: one eighteen feet long and another thirty-five feet in length. These Snakes when at liberty are ravenous and dangerous, and will seize animals of large size, and after crushing them so as to break all their bones, will swallow them whole. The crew of the Planet report that the largest of these Snakes had devoured a woman and child before it was taken. On Saturday they were preparing to feed it with a good sized dog."—New York Commercial Advertiser.
The above enormous Snakes are now on

EXHIBITION AT THIS MUSEUM

No Serpent bearing any comparison in point of colossal proportions to

These Extraordinary Monsters!

Have ever been imported before into this country—all Anacondas and Boa Constrictors heretofore seen in America, huge as some have been,

SHRINK INTO MERE WORMS
In the presence of the leviathan of this collection.

One of these large Snakes has nearly doubled his proportions, having on Saturday last

☞ Swallowed 8 Pigs and 3 Rabbits

In presence of Hundreds of Visitors. The other large Snake is

EXPECTED HOURLY TO FEED

The Greatest Living Human Phenomenons
Now to be seen throughout the Day and Evening at this establishment, viz: the

LIVING SKELETON

MR. R. O. WICKWARE, The Second Calvin Edson is now here, being

THE THINNEST MAN IN THE WORLD,
With limbs, only ONE INCH IN DIAMETER—A wonderful curiosity.

SMALLEST WOMAN IN THE WORLD.

MISS ELIZABETH REID is a native of Philadelphia, well educated and intelligent, is 18 years of age, a little less than 3 feet in height, and weighs 29 pounds. She is a fully developed woman, being perfectly proportioned in form and feature, and may truthfully be pronounced the SMALLEST female DWARF in existence. It does seem as if Nature has been partial especially to this little MINIATURE OF HUMANITY, and so has given her a very beautiful face and form. She is as graceful and majestic as a Queen

MAY CARLETON'S LAST TRIUMPH!

A TALE OF DEEP AND THRILLING INTEREST,

Gipsy Gower

OR THE

STAR OF THE VALLEY!

A TALE OF MYSTERY IN NEW YORK AND THE MIDDLE STATES,

By COUSIN MAY CARLETON

Author of "The Rover Chief," "Edith Percival," Etc.

IS COMMENCED IN THE

New York Mercury

FOR SATURDAY, NOVEMBER 5, 1859.

Like all the Stories of the talented young American Autoress, COUSIN MAY CARLETON, "GIPSY GOWER" will be found of the most intensely thrilling character. The wild and unfathomable mystery that surrounds "Gipsy," the heroine, is of itself almost a miracle of art, and will hold the reader spell-bound to the very last chapter.

THE NEW YORK MERCURY is the largest, handsomest, and most beautifully illustrated story paper in the world. It has the best writers and is all original. Felix O. C. Darley illustrates its Tales and Romances. BAYARD TAYLOR writes only for the MERCURY, and his new letters from California will shortly commence. All Postmasters receive Subscriptions for the MERCURY, and many sell it by the single copy. Terms, $2.00 a Year, Three Copies, $5.00, Eight Copies, $12.00, with an extra Copy gratis. Six Months Subscription received. Specimens sent Free.

CAULDWELL, SOUTHWORTH & WHITNEY, Proprietors,
22 Spruce Street, New York City.

B. RATHBUN
CARRIAGE MANUFACTURER
BUFFALO.

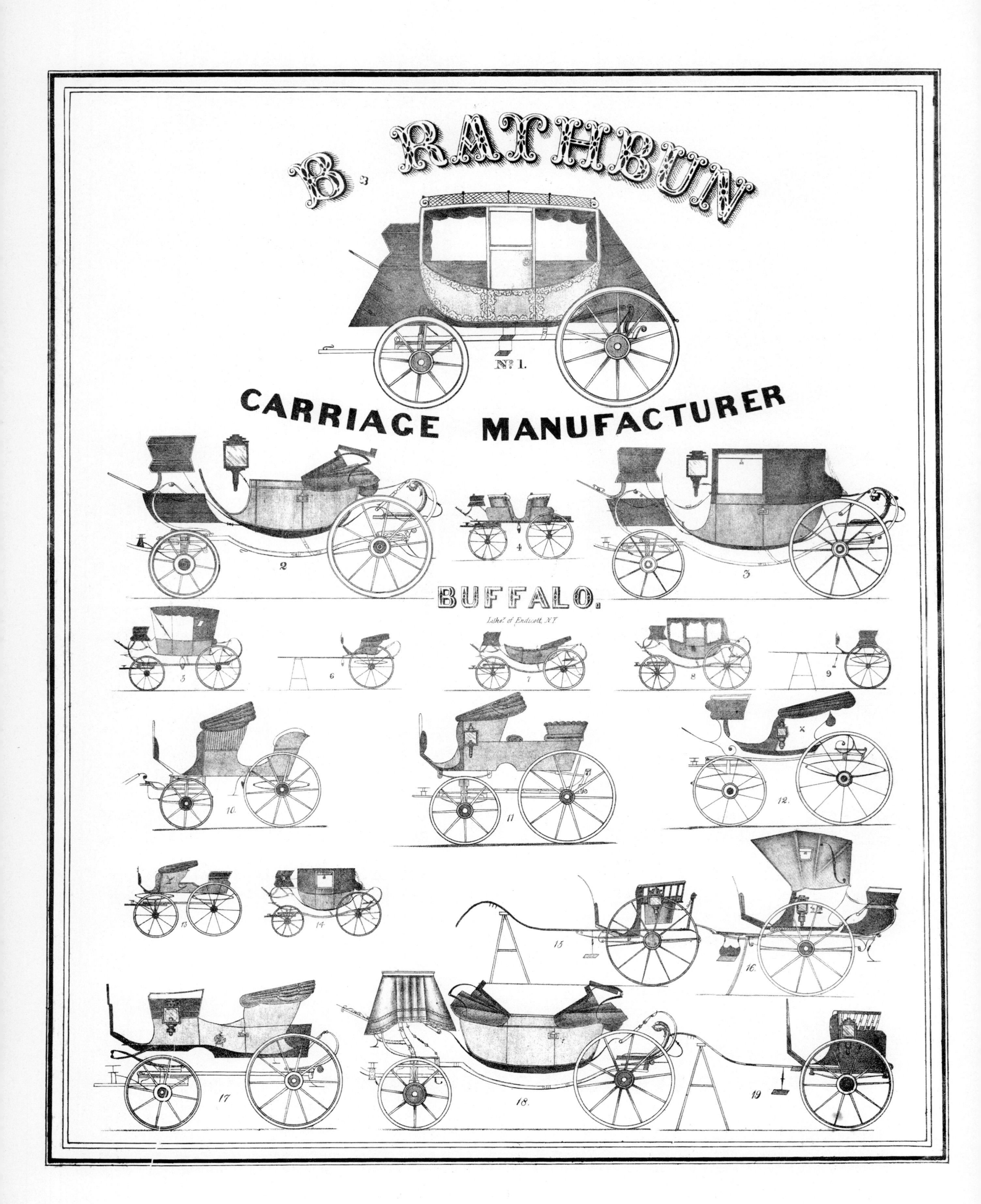

Westchester Stove Works
Office & Sales Room
No. 69 Warren St. N. York.

We would beg to introduce ourselves to your notice as manufacturers of Stoves, Ranges, Furnaces &c. as proprietors of the Westchester Stove Works, Westchester Co. New York.

The patterns which we offer are new, and especially selected with a view to utility, simplicity in operation, and perfectness in construction and durability.

Our terms are the same as govern the general trade in both credits and discounts.

For convenience in shipping we are not excelled by any works of the kind, either by sea, river or railroad transit.

We intend to pay direct attention to the requirements of the trade and to merit that confidence which a faithful fulfilment of our promises will protect.

Respectfully,
New, Ewell & Co.

Foundry, Westchester Co. N.Y.

Elizabethan Parlor — 4 Sizes for Wood & Coal.

Home Companion No. 7 & 8. This will be found to be the most Condensed and satisfactory Cooking Apparatus yet introduced.

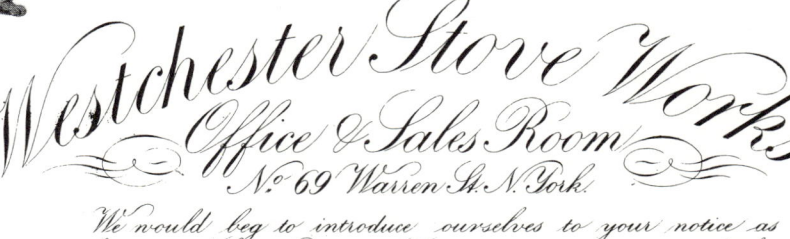

Radiator (Parlor) — 4 Sizes for Coal.

Crown of the West No. 7 & 9. Has a long fire-box and large oven. Designed for Wood.

Woodland Farmer No. 8 & 9.

Cottage Home No. 6, 7, 8 & 9. Designed for Wood.

Princess No. 7, 8 & 9. for Coal.

Uncle Tom No. 5, 5½, 6 & 7. for Coal.

Connecticut No. 6, 7 & 8. for Wood or Coal.

Peace Maker 5 Sizes, 16, 18, 20, 22 & 24 inch fire-box.

Continental No. 7 & 8. for Coal or Wood.

For sale in _____ By _____

BEAUTIFULLY ILLUMINATED SHOW CARDS FOR EVERY BUSINESS,
BY
SHEARMAN & HART
PRACTICAL
LITHOGRAPHERS.
FULTON 99 STREET
CORNER OF WILLIAM
NEW YORK.
SCHOOL CERTIFICATES, DIPLOMAS, &c. &c.
PAPER WRAPPERS, LETTER HEADINGS, CARDS, FAC SIMILE CIRCULARS, &c. &c.
ORNAMENTAL DESIGNS, FANCY BORDERS.
MAPS, PLANS, BILL HEADS, LABELS, ENGRAVED CIRCULARS.
SHOW CARDS for JEWELLERS, SILVER PLATERS &c.
SHOW CARDS for PIANO MAKERS, MUSIC TITLES &c.
BOOT & SHOE MAKERS, LEATHER FINISHERS &c.
SHOW CARDS for FURNITURE MANUF RS &c.
SHOW CARDS for FACTORIES, FOUNDRIES
SHOW CARDS for SEWING MACHINE
SHOW CARDS for HATTERS, HAT CIRCULARS &c.
VIEWS of RESIDENCES, LANDSCAPES, CITIES &c.
SHOW CARDS for HARDWARE STORES
SHOW CARDS for CLOTHIERS
STEAMSHIPS, STEAMBOATS
SHOW CARDS for LIVERY STABLES, CARRIAGE MAKERS &c.
SHOW CARDS & CALENDERS for STATIONERS &c.
VIEWS of HOTELS, CHURCHES, PUBLIC BUILDINGS &c.
SHOW CARDS for PERFUMERY, FANCY GOODS &c.
PORTRAITS, GROUPS, PROCESSIONS, CARDS &c.

COLT'S PATENT FIRE ARMS MANUFACTORY,
HARTFORD, CONN.

MECHANIC'S HALL.
PAVILION AT THE STATE AGRICULTURAL FAIR ALBANY N.Y. 1850.
RALPH & CO.
PROPRIETORS OF THE
UNION AGRICULTURAL WORKS
AND
MANUFACTURERS & DEALERS
at WHOLESALE & RETAIL in
FARMING IMPLEMENTS
& MACHINERY.
WAREHOUSE & SEED-STORE
23 Fulton Street.
NEW-YORK.
Ed. RALPH, Jr. L.S. HOYT, H.R. WESTERVELT.
DESIGNED & DRAWN BY FORBES, ALBANY.
UNION AGRICULTURAL WAREHOUSE & SEED STORE.
RALPH & CO.
RALPH & CO.
UNION AGRICULTURAL WORKS.
EMERY & CO.
LITH. OF R. H. PEASE, ALBANY.
EMERY & CO'S
IMPROVED RAIL ROAD HORSE POWER & OVER SHOT THRESHER

GEORGE HART
PLAIN & ORNAMENTAL
SLATE ROOFER.
54
ROOSEVELT ST.
NEW YORK.
METAL
CORNICES
Slates of all Shapes and Colors furnished and put on in the best manner.
Slate and Tin Roofs repaired, Gutters, Leaders & Cornices made and put up, by George Hart.
The attention of ARCHITECTS, BUILDERS, and all others interested in the erection of CHURCHES, VILLAS, COTTAGES &c. is respectfully called to these New Styles of SLATE ROOFING, which add so much to the Beauty and Finish of the Building.
Washington.
Octagon.
American Cottage.
Plain.
LITH. IN COLORS BY SHEARMAN & HART 99 FULTON ST. N.Y.

New-York Historical Society.
Lectures on Egypt: 1864.

CONCLUDING LECTURE BY

PROF. HENRY J. ANDERSON, LL. D.,
HALL OF THE UNION, COOPER INSTITUTE,

Thursday, December 15th, at 7½ o'clock, P. M.,

To be followed by the

Unrolling of the Mummy.

TICKETS . . . 50 CENTS.

JOHN O'BRIEN'S
SIX SHOWS CONSOLIDATED!

The **GORGEOUS PARADE** in all its Glory will pass through the streets forming

A Dazzling Array of Splendor
Unapproached and unapproachable.

A KALEIDOSCOPIC CORTEGE
Resplendent in Gildings, Mirrors, Paintings, Carvings and Glittering Sheen, Gorgeous with Banners and Heralded by Music without a parallel in all the World.

3 CHARIOTS
Of ponderous bulk and massive proportions, of exquisite designs and peculiar construction, will be Drawn by

Hundreds of English Horses
And Teams of Andulasian Mules, followed by Gigantic Elephants from Asia, and a Caravan of Camels.

3 BRASS BANDS
Directed by **PROF. KAUFFMAN**

53 IRON GIRDED PALACE DENS
OF **CAPTIVE WILD BEASTS**
The Largest and most valuable Collection on Exhibition under the Sun.

MUSEUM VANS
Containing Curiosities from Earth, Sea and Air, at once Impressive, Instructive and Amusing.

BE IN TOWN EARLY
That you may not miss the sight which once seen can never be forgotten.

JAMES REILLEY.

ADMISSION	50 CENTS
Children under 9 years of age	25 Cents

Doors open at 1 and 7 P. M.   Commence at 2 and 8 o'clock, P. M.

James Reilley, Printer and Engraver, 12, 14 and 16 Spruce Street, New York,

WILL EXHIBIT AT

THE ORIGINAL AND WORLD FAMED
WILD WEST
AND GREAT
FOREPAUGH SHOWS
SENSATIONAL AND STARTLING REPRODUCTION OF
GEN. CUSTER'S MEMORABLE BATTLE OF THE LITTLE BIG HORN!

WHAT THE People Want IS A Place to Go AND SOMETHING TO SEE

IT IS AN Absolute Fact That more people from a distance attend the Forepaugh Show than any other Exhibition in existence. Railway officials recognize this important truth, and not only arrange **SPECIAL EXCURSIONS** And supply extra trains, but invariably instruct all Station Agents to make diligent inquiries as to the number of people that are likely to visit the Great Show, so that sufficient cars can be provided.

THE Atrocious MOUNTAIN MEADOW MASSACRE.

POSITIVELY THE MOST NOVEL AND Gigantic Exhibition EVER PRESENTED.
WILD WEST
HIPPODROME
CUSTER BATTLE
Mountain Meadow Massacre
GRAND CIRCUS
Museum and Menagerie
ALL COMBINED FOR 1888

ADAM FOREPAUGH JR'S BLONDIN HORSE

Where to Go AND HOW TO Get THERE SEE OPPOSITE SIDE of THIS BILL

FEMALE LARIAT THROWERS.

LADY BUCKING HORSE RIDERS.

SHOOTING FROM HORSEBACK.   BREAKING GLASS BALLS THROWN IN DIFFERENT POSITIONS.

The RECONSTRUCTED and ONLY GREAT WILD WEST SHOW COMING THIS SEASON, IS NOW COMBINED WITH ADAM FOREPAUGH'S
Genuine Indians.   Real Soldiers and Scouts.
Emigrants Crossing the Prairie.
Custer's Battle and Mountain Meadow Massacre.

Realistic Attack on the Overland Mail!
Sharp Shooting.   Round Ups.   Lassoing Real Buffalo by Genuine Cow-Boys.   Fort Life in the Far West.
Virginia Reel on Horseback.   Frontier Life in all its Phases.

MORRELL SHOW PRINT, 611-613 ARCH ST., PHILAD'A.

Dale Manufacturing Company
PATERSON, N.J.

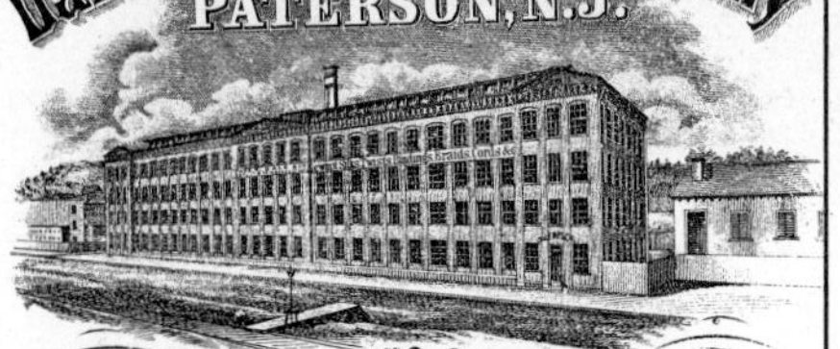

SEWING SILK
MACHINE TWIST, BUTTON HOLE TWIST, BINDINGS, BRAIDS, GALLOONS &c. &c.
DEPOT
Tho's. N. Dale & Co.
Importers & Manufacturers
(O F)
Clothiers & Tailors Trimmings.
N.os 17 & 19 Warren St.
NEW YORK.

THO'S N. DALE
GEO. RICHMOND
JOHN R. HARRIS
JOS. H. BROWN

61 West 4th St. Cincinnati
610 Chestnut St. Philadelphia
8 Rue Neuve St. Augustin Paris

H. W. STEHR & CO.
CLOTHS,
Cassimeres, Vestings &c.
76 READE STREET
near Broadway, NEW YORK.
H. W. STEHR | C. LUDEKE.

G. H. WITTHAUS & Co.
Importers & Manufacturers
OF FINE MENS
FURNISHING GOODS
SUITABLE FOR
FASHIONABLE MERCHANT TAILORS TRADE
318 Broadway, NEW YORK
G. H. WITTHAUS G. J. WITTHAUS C. W. TOPHAM

BERNHEIMER & NEWMAN
IMPORTERS & MANUFACTURERS OF
TAILORS TRIMMINGS
Hosiery & Gents Furnishing Goods
87 Chambers & 69 Reade Sts.
NEW YORK.
SOLE AGENTS for the O.K. SILK MILLS, in
PATERSON, N.J.

Cha.s Beardslee, Bro.s & Co.
N.o 102 New Number 403 North Main St.
ST LOUIS, M.O.
IMPORTERS AND WHOLESALE DEALERS IN
CLOTHS CASSIMERES VESTINGS & PIECE GOODS
OF ALL KINDS FOR
Mens Wear and Tailors Trimmings
CHAS. BEARDSLEE, New York. REUBEN BEARDSLEE, Chicago. PHINEAS BEARDSLEE, St. Louis.

SUPPLEMENT TO FASHIONS FOR 1867-68, BY H. CLAYS, N.o 8 JOHN S.t N.Y.

CHA.s BEARDSLEE, BRO.s & Co.
N.o 56 LAKE ST.
CHICAGO.
ILLINOIS.
Importers and Wholesale Dealers in
CLOTHS CASSIMERES VESTINGS AND PIECE GOODS
OF ALL KINDS FOR
MENS WEAR AND TAILORS TRIMMINGS.
CHAS. BEARDSLEE, NEW YORK. REUBEN BEARDSLEE CHICAGO
PHINEAS BEARDSLEE, ST LOUIS. C. W. A. BIDDLE D.o

HINCK BROTHERS
CLOTH HOUSE
398 Broadway
Corn. Walker St. NEW YORK.

Carhart, Whitford & Co.
Manufacturers & Wholesale Dealers
(IN)
FINE CLOTHING,
AMERICAN EXPRESS BUILDING
55, 57, 59 & 61 Hudson St.
near Duane
NEW YORK.
E. T. CARHART
W. H. WHITFORD
J. B. VAN WAGENEN
A. T. HAMILTON

Weaver, Richardson & Co.
IMPORTERS & DEALERS
IN
WOOLENS,
AND GOODS ADAPTED TO MEN'S WEAR,
66 & 68 Reade St.
Near Broadway NEW YORK.
PHILIP G. WEAVER,
WM. RICHARDSON,
WM. M. WOODHULL,
R. S. VAN TASSEL,
EDWARD BRADLEY,

MERRILL & Co.
IMPORTERS AND MANUFACTURERS OF
CLOTHIERS & TAILORS
TRIMMINGS
34 Warren Str.
NEW YORK.
AGENTS FOR GEO. R. SKINNER'S MACHINE TWIST.

The Worlds great want!!
BUTTON'S
THAT NEVER COME OFF

REED'S PATENT FRICTION
REVOLVING BUTTON RIVETTER.
PRICE
ONLY 15 DOLLARS!!
One Girl's work equal to 12 Men!!
Please call or direct orders to the Company's Office
U. S. PAT BUTTON RIVET &c. MFG. CO.
N.o 110 Leonard St. NEW YORK.

HORSWELL, KINSLEY & FRENCH
IMPORTERS OF
FINE WOOLENS
12 & 14 SUMMER ST.
BOSTON.

Lesher, Whitman & Co.
IMPORTERS OF
CLOTHIERS
TRIMMINGS
279, 281 & 283, BROADWAY.
NEW YORK.
S. R. LESHER
N. WHITMAN
G. H. DUNHAM
AGENTS FOR THE NEPPERHAN SILK MILLS.

BRAINERD & ARMSTRONG
IMPORTERS & DEALERS IN
SEWING SILK MACHINE TWIST
Tailors Trimmings &c.
469 BROADWAY
NEW YORK.
J. P. BRAINERD
B. A. ARMSTRONG

RUNK & WHITE

YOUTHS, BOYS AND CHILDRENS CLOTHING
WHOLESALE
398 Broadway,
CORN. WALKER ST. NEW YORK

THE
ELECTRIC EXTRACTOR
THE ELECTRIC
No. 1
EXTRACTOR
For Removing
Paint, Oil, Tar, Varnish
Grease, Ink and Fruit
Stains from Garments
and all Silk, Woolen &
Linen fabrics.
PERFECTLY ODORLESS.
THE
ELECTRIC EXTRACTOR COMPY
DIRECTIONS
Apply with sponge or Cloth
PRICE 25c 50c & $1.00
For Sale by all Druggists
Pat. by C.B. SKIFF.
June 22 1869.
PATENTED
June 22nd 1869
by
C. B. SKIFF.
Entered according to Act of Congress in the year
1869 by C.B. SKIFF in the Clerks office of
the Dist Court of the U.S. of the Dist of
New Jersey
FOR SALE HERE.
M. F. BRAISTED,
PREST.
C. O. MANNY,
CASHR.
LITH IN COLORS
by CHAS HART, 99 & 101 FULTON ST.
N.Y.

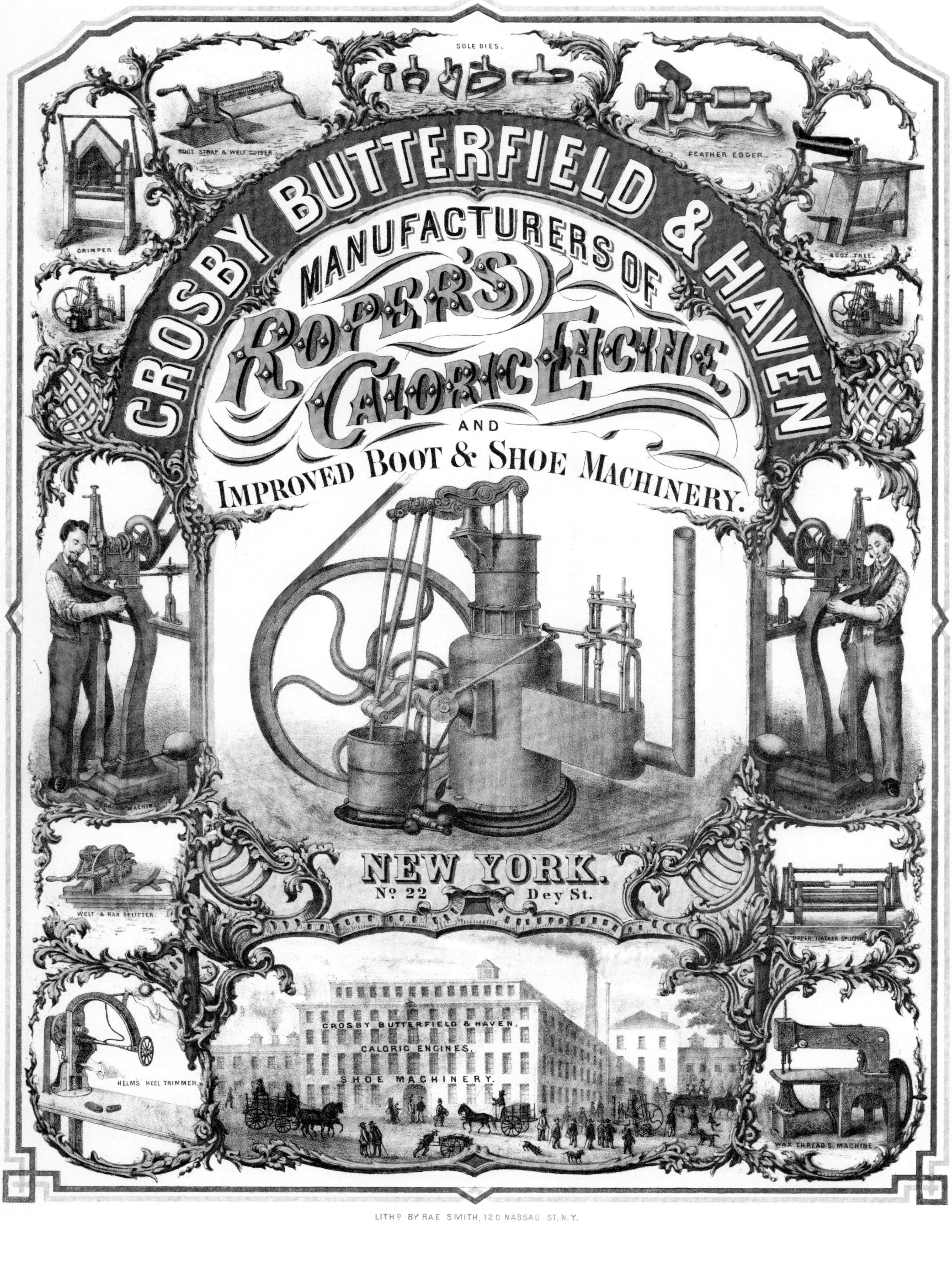

LITH° BY RAE SMITH, 120 NASSAU ST. N.Y.

SPRING STYLES
409
TERRY
HATS & FURS.
JOHN R. TERRY, HATTER
INFANTS.
1. JOCKIE.
6. LE BIJOU.
2. FLONTA.
4. STAR.
5. VASCO.
3. ROSETTE.
LADIES & MISSES.
13. VESTA.
16. PAREPA
15. PATTI
7. RISTORI.
14. SUNDOWN.
9. QUEEN.
8. ALMA.
11. ENG. TURBAN.
12. HENRIETTA.
10. FRENCH TURBAN.
17. CINDRELLON.
BOY'S & YOUTH'S.
1867.
23. FLEETWING.
22. JEROME.
21. CROQUET.
18. JOCKIE.
20. HENRIETTA.
24. VESTA.
25. STRAW JOCKIE.
19. ENG. CAP.
MEN'S.
36. DERBY.
28. BROADWAY.
37. DERBY FLAT.
42. BISMARK.
30. BLK. CROOK.
39. DRESS 3×2
27. PARIS.
43. HENRIETTA.
26. LONDON.
41. HEMP.
38. DRESS 4×2½.
31. FLEETWING.
33. CROQUET.
29. ENGLISH.
34. PANAMA.
35. PANAMA FLAT.
40. GEN. GRANT.
J. R. TERRY,
Importer, Manufacturer, Wholesale & Retail Dealer in
GENT'S, BOY'S, YOUTH'S,
Ladies, Misses & Childrens
HATS, CAPS, FURS
and STRAWGOODS.
409 BROADWAY,
NEW YORK.
THE MAJOR & KNAPP ENG. MFG. & LITH. CO. 71 BROADWAY, N.Y.

INDIAN COMPOUND
OF
HONEY BONESET
AND
SQUILLS.
FOR COUGHS, COLDS, AND ALL AFFECTIONS
OF THE
THROAT AND LUNGS.
FOR SALE HERE.

Lith. of Chas. Hart, 99 Fulton St. N.Y.

THE CELEBRATED
WILD CHERRY
TONIC!
FOR THE CURE OF
ALL NERVOUS DISORDERS, DYSPEPSIA,
JAUNDICE,
BILIOUS COMPLAINTS
LOSS OF APPETITE & GENERAL DEBILITY.

PREPARED BY M. K. PAINE,
Druggist & Apothecary, - - - WINDSOR, VT.

SOLD HERE.

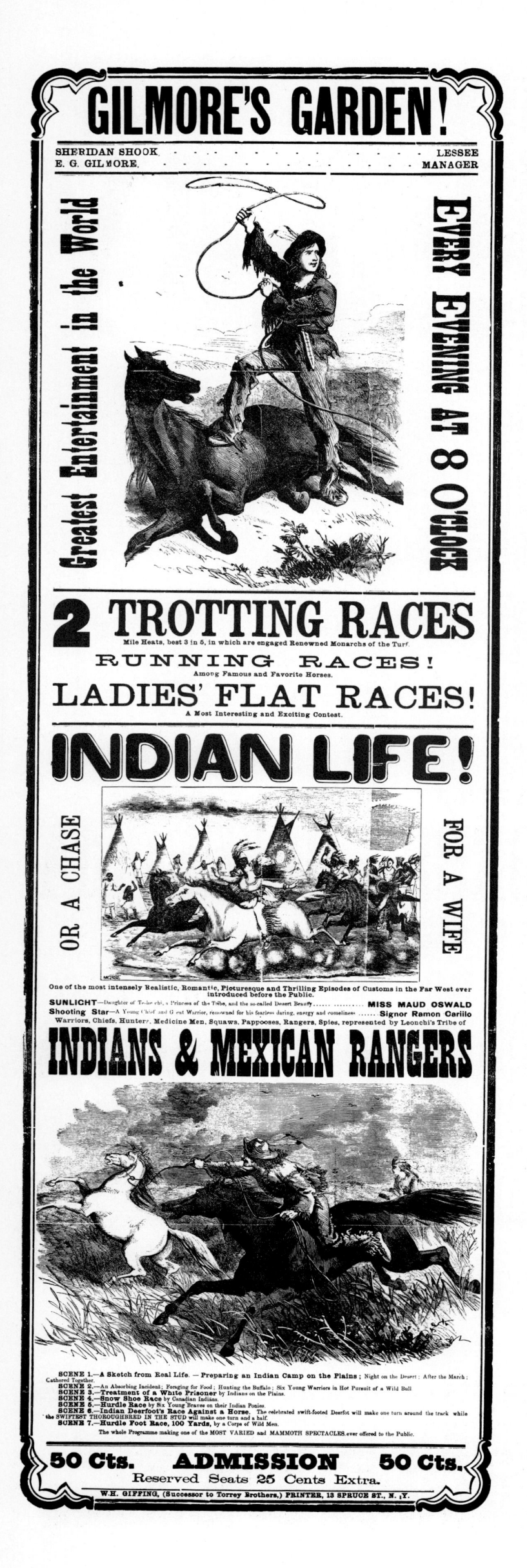

GILMORE'S GARDEN!

SHERIDAN SHOOK .... LESSEE
E. G. GILMORE .... MANAGER

Greatest Entertainment in the World

EVERY EVENING AT 8 O'CLOCK

2 TROTTING RACES
Mile Heats, best 3 in 5, in which are engaged Renowned Monarchs of the Turf.

RUNNING RACES!
Among Famous and Favorite Horses.

LADIES' FLAT RACES!
A Most Interesting and Exciting Contest.

INDIAN LIFE!

OR A CHASE — **FOR A WIFE**

One of the most intensely Realistic, Romantic, Picturesque and Thrilling Episodes of Customs in the Far West ever introduced before the Public.

SUNLIGHT—Daughter of To-lo-chi, a Princess of the Tribe, and the so-called Desert Beauty .... MISS MAUD OSWALD
Shooting Star—A Young Chief and Great Warrior, renowned for his fearless daring, energy and coolness .... Signor Ramon Carillo
Warriors, Chiefs, Hunters, Medicine Men, Squaws, Pappooses, Rangers, Spies, represented by Leonchi's Tribe of

INDIANS & MEXICAN RANGERS

SCENE 1.—A Sketch from Real Life.—Preparing an Indian Camp on the Plains; Night on the Desert; After the March; Gathered Together.
SCENE 2.—An Absorbing Incident; Foraging for Food; Hunting the Buffalo; Six Young Warriors in Hot Pursuit of a Wild Bull.
SCENE 3.—Treatment of a White Prisoner by Indians on the Plains.
SCENE 4.—Snow Shoe Race by Canadian Indians.
SCENE 5.—Hurdle Race by Six Young Braves on their Indian Ponies.
SCENE 6.—Indian Deerfoot's Race Against a Horse. The celebrated swift-footed Deerfoot will make one turn around the track while the SWIFTEST THOROUGHBRED IN THE STUD will make one turn and a half.
SCENE 7.—Hurdle Foot Race, 100 Yards, by a Corps of Wild Men.

The whole Programme making one of the MOST VARIED and MAMMOTH SPECTACLES ever offered to the Public.

50 Cts.   ADMISSION   50 Cts.
Reserved Seats 25 Cents Extra.

W. H. GIFFING, (Successor to Torrey Brothers,) PRINTER, 13 SPRUCE ST., N.Y.

WOOD'S MUSEUM
NEW YORK.

COMMENCING MONDAY EVE'G, NOVEMBER 11th, 1872,
SIX NIGHTS AND SATURDAY MATINEE.

J. M. Ward as Buffalo Bill!

FRED. G. MAEDER'S GREAT DRAMA, FROM NED BUNTLINE'S WEEKLY STORY.

BUFFALO BILL!

KING OF THE BORDER MEN!

PLAYED EIGHT WEEKS IN NEW YORK.

150,000 PEOPLE ENDORSE IT.

GREAT BORDER STORY!

PRAIRIE ON FIRE, &c.   INDIAN SOCIETY DRAMA

Life on the Plains!   **Western Perils!**

BUFFALO BILL MATINEE SATURDAY!   FRIDAY, J. M. WARD'S BENEFIT!

MERRIHEW & SON, Steam-Power Show Printers, 135 N. Third St., Phila.

"Vrolyke Kersthd! Gelukkig Nieuwjaar!"
1877—1878

Entered according to Act of Congress, in the year 1873, by C. F. A. HINRICHS, in the Office of the Librarian of Congress, at Washington.

ESTABLISHED 1801

C. F. A. HINRICHS,
Toys, Glass, Fancy Goods
WHOLESALE AND RETAIL,
29 to 31 PARK PLACE, N.Y.

I PLEAD FOR ALL.
I RULE FOR ALL.
1776.
E PLURIBUS
UNUM
1876.
I FIGHT FOR ALL.
I PREACH FOR ALL.
I CARRY FOR ALL.
I FEED YOU ALL.
I SAIL FOR ALL.
BOARD OF TRADE
GENERAL BROKERAGE.
I BULL & BEAR FOR ALL.
I FLEECE YOU ALL.
I PHYSIC YOU ALL.
I BUY & SELL FOR ALL.

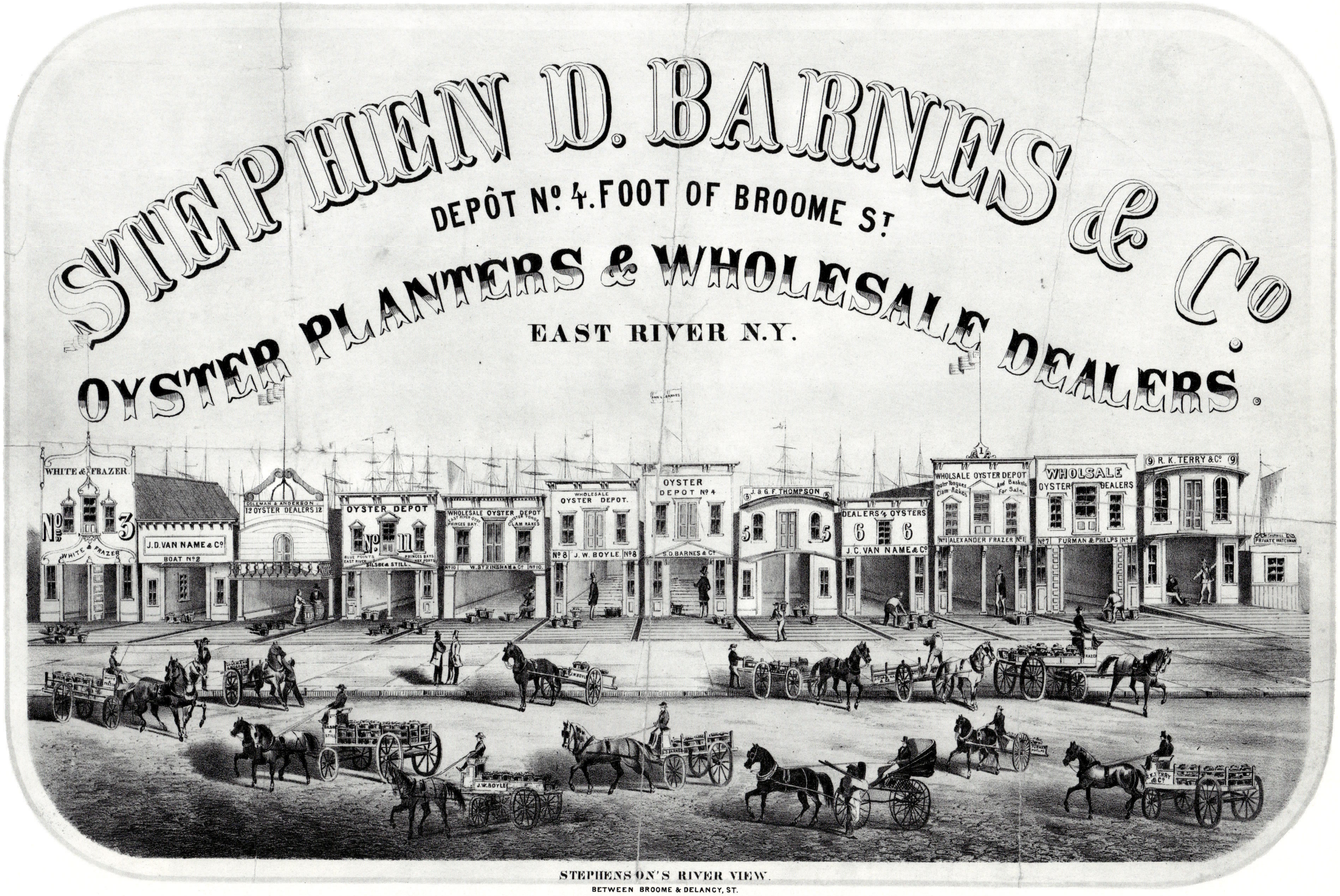

STEPHENSON'S RIVER VIEW.
BETWEEN BROOME & DELANCY, ST.

EAST STREET, N.Y.

TRY RICE'S SEEDS

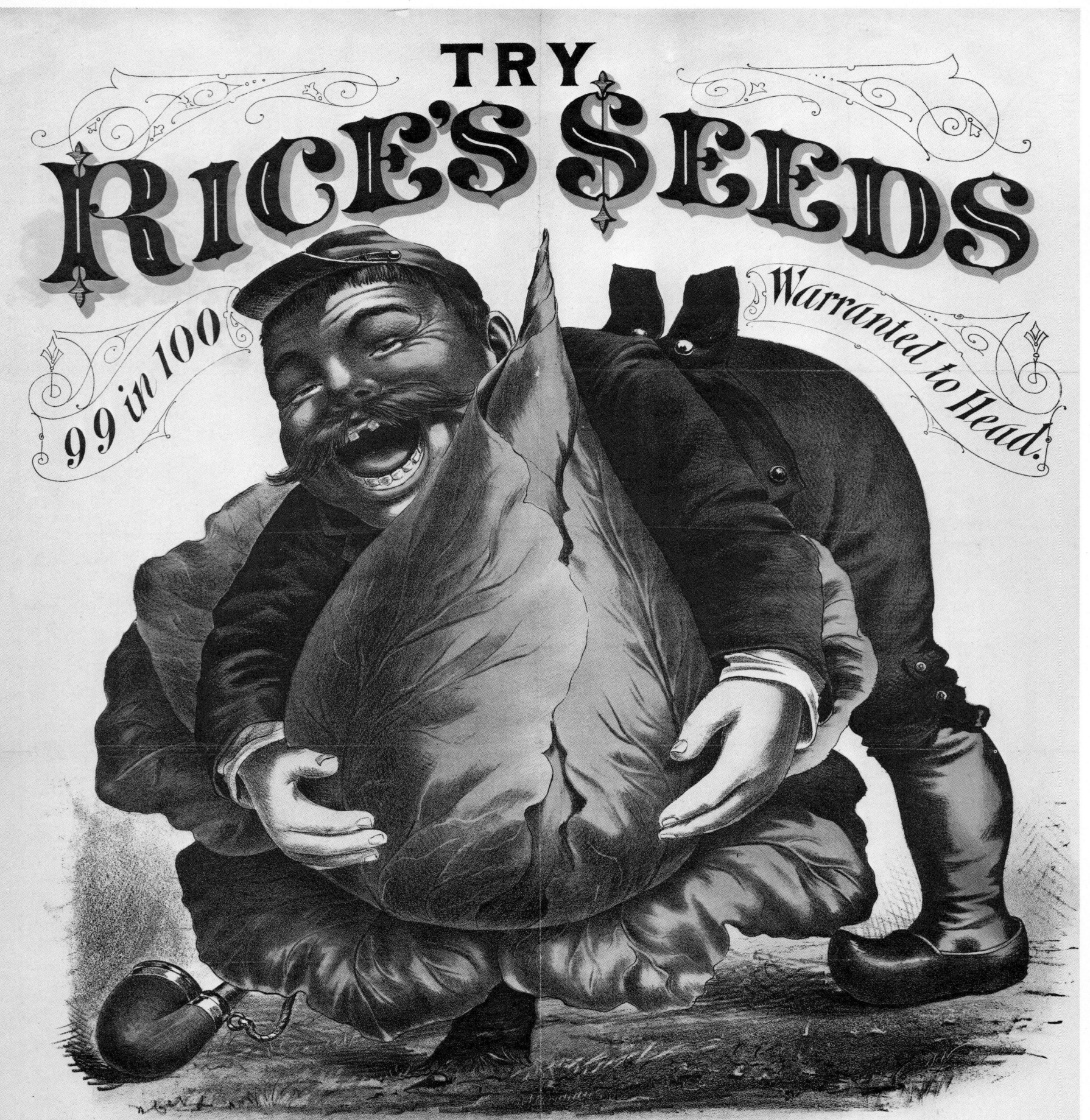

99 in 100 — *Warranted to Head.*

THIS VARIETY IS NOT AFFECTED BY THE CABBAGE WORM,

True Early Winningstadt
THE BEST CABBAGE IN THE WORLD
GROWN BY JEROME B. RICE,
At the Cambridge Valley Seed Gardens, Cambridge, N.Y.

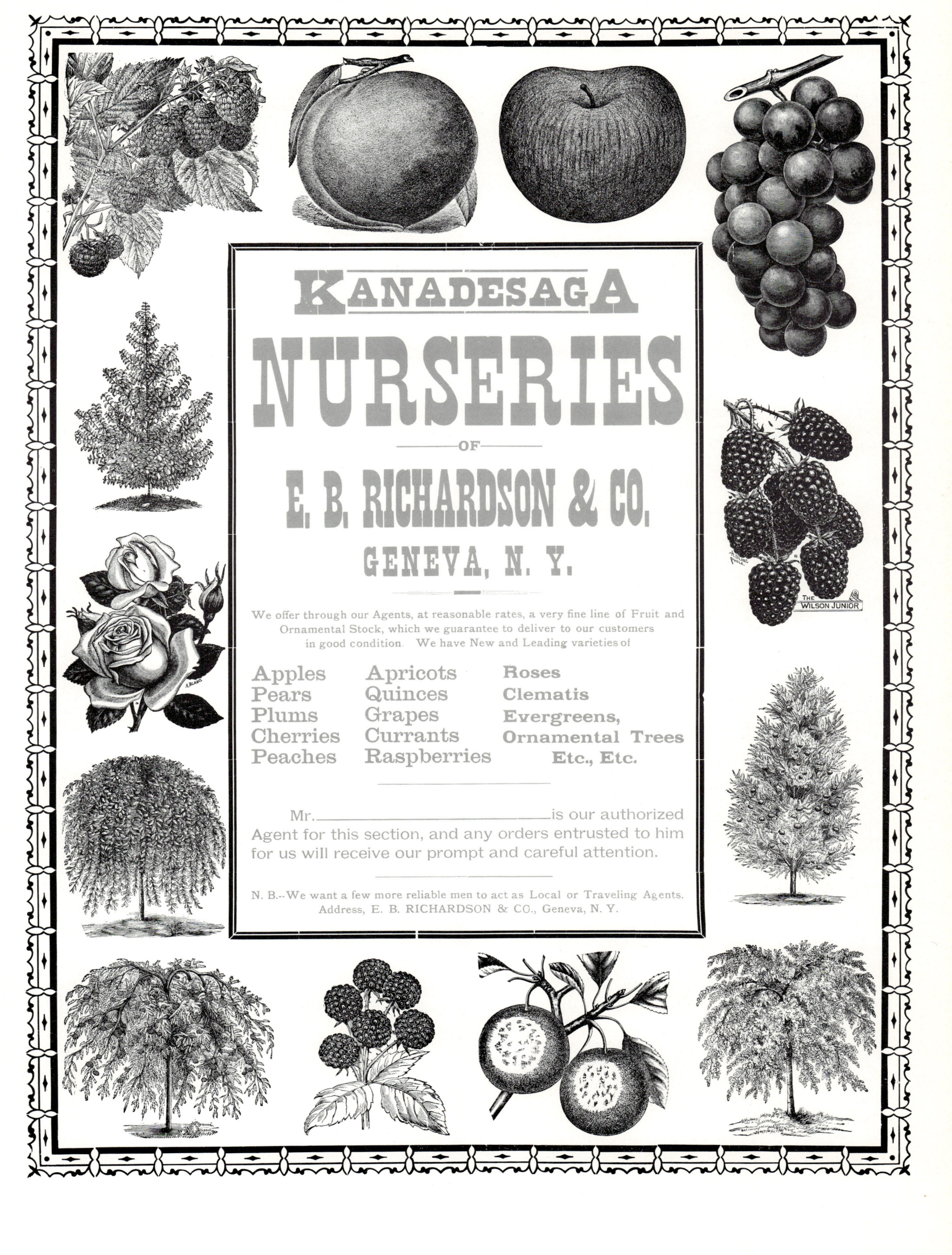

KANADESAGA
NURSERIES
OF
E. B. RICHARDSON & CO.
GENEVA, N. Y.

We offer through our Agents, at reasonable rates, a very fine line of Fruit and Ornamental Stock, which we guarantee to deliver to our customers in good condition. We have New and Leading varieties of

Apples	Apricots	Roses
Pears	Quinces	Clematis
Plums	Grapes	Evergreens,
Cherries	Currants	Ornamental Trees
Peaches	Raspberries	Etc., Etc.

Mr._____ is our authorized Agent for this section, and any orders entrusted to him for us will receive our prompt and careful attention.

N. B.--We want a few more reliable men to act as Local or Traveling Agents. Address, E. B. RICHARDSON & CO., Geneva, N. Y.

EDW. RIDLEY & SONS

MILLINERY, & FANCY GOODS

STRAW GOODS

Sole Manufacturers of the
IMPERIAL PANAMA, LEGHORN, TAPE & CHIP HATS.

THE ABOVE SHAPES ARE MADE IN FRENCH AND SWISS CHIPS, MILAN, PEDAL, PEARL, COBURG, CANTON WHITE BLACK AND IMITATION HAIR, IN ALL COLORS AND COMBINATIONS, &c.

IN ORDERING, PLEASE STATE MATERIAL, COLOR, NAME AND NUMBER OF SHAPE.

TRIMMED HATS
Second Floor
309, 311 & 311½
GRAND ST.

Accessible by Elevators.
NEW YORK.

HATS TRIMMED TO ORDER
Fourth Floor.
58, 60, 62, 64, 66, 68 & 70
ALLEN ST.

Entrance 62 & 64 Allen Street.

"THE OLD" AND "THE NEW"

THE WOMAN'S FRIEND

Look here, Weary Woman, there is Rest for You!
STEAM WILL DO YOUR WASHING!

THE STEAM WASHER
OR
WOMAN'S FRIEND.
PRICE, - $10.00.

The Latest, the Cheapest, the Best---No Rubbing, no Pounding, no Turning or Tearing, no clumsy Cylinder, and no $20 or $30 expense. Steam does it all! Nothing like it in use. Call and see it in operation.

AT _____ Or Address J. C. Tilton, Patentee, Pittsburgh, Pa.

A FEW SPECIAL AGENTS WANTED!
A GOOD OPENING FOR MEN OUT OF EMPLOYMENT WHO REALLY WANT TO MAKE MONEY.

SPECIAL AND GENERAL AGENT.

JOHN JACOBIN AND HIS WIFE JANE ON WASH DAY.

JANE:
"I'll tell you what it is, John, I cannot wash to-day,
This cruel, clumsy wash-board will wear my life away;
So you had better start now and tell the widow Meek
That she will have to wash for me one day in every week."

JOHN:
"How often must I say, Jane, that I'm too cruel poor
To hire all our washing; I'll tell you now once more.
Just look at Sally White there, a little puny thing—
She does her washing all herself—you ought to hear her sing.
She does not dread the wash-board, but sings its gloom away,
And hangs her clothes out on the line quite early in the day.
She never scolds her husband—she always bakes no sour bread;
These both you do, (I'm loth to say,) till I am nearly dead."

JANE:
"If you was like Bill White, John, I'd have no cruel fate,
And I've a mind this minute, to break your pumpkin pate!
Bill White's a man of mercy; he always churns the cream;
He's bought his wife a wash-machine that washes clothes by steam.
"It is the new 'Steam Washer,' they call the 'Woman's Friend,'
Got up by J. C. Tilton, this horrid drudge to end.

While Sally's washing dishes, her clothes by steam are done;
She hangs them out to dry by nine, and irons them at one.

"I tell you it's the thing, John, just grumble as you may,
And you have got to buy me one, or leave on washing day;
I'll make it hot and heavy, and lecture you all night,
But buy the 'Woman's Friend' for me, I'll sing like Sally White."

JOHN:
"Do tell me what you mean, Jane, by talking in that way:
You surely do not fancy I'm able now to pay
A hundred dollars certain—perhaps as many more,
To buy a great steam engine that's nothing but a bore?

"You wash by steam! Alas! Jane, where would the engine set?
You have so little room now you're always in a fret.
That horrid J. C. Tilton, should he bring one around,
I surely should insult him bad—perhaps his noggin pound.

"Where did you ever see one? What is it like, I pray?
As big as our smoke-house, or yonder stack of hay?
'Twould tear the clothes to pieces—we've none too many now;
Our kitchen is too small for it, (thank fortune,) anyhow."

JANE:
"John Jacobin, you numskull! I once thought you was wise,
But I have changed my mind on this—you shock me with surprise!
The Washer is a little thing to set upon the stove,
So light that little Minnie, there, could easily remove.

"'Tis easy, quite, to buy one—ten dollars is the price;
It is so neat and handy, and washes clothes so nice.
You ask me where I'd set it?—why under yonder bed;
Will this dispel the silly whims within your pumpkin head?

"It tears the clothes to pieces! Well, John, I do declare,
The price you have to pay for it 'twill rave within a year.
Ten dollars' worth of clothing each year is rubbed away
On this detested wash-board here. What more have you to say?

"The 'Woman's Friend' will save this; no rubbing need you do.
The rinsing is the only work a woman has to do;
And if she has a wringer, her task will soon be o'er.
So buy the 'Woman's Friend' for me, I'll scold you then no more.

"Then I will go to Sally, and learn that pretty song
We heard her sing the other day, as we did ride along.

I'll learn it—yes I will, John—and sing the live-long day,
Like Sally White, and never scold; so, now, what can you say?"

JOHN:
"I'll tell you what it is, Jane, just promise, right away,
That you will sing like Sally White on every washing day,
And never bake me sour bread, and will your temper mend,
I'll go to J. C. Tilton now, and buy the 'Woman's Friend.'"

JANE:
"I will, I will, I will, John, and seal it with a kiss;
But now, before the bargain's closed, you, too, must promise this:
That you will on each washing day churn butter from the cream,
While I sit in the rocking chair and wash the clothes by steam.

"This, too, I wish to add John, that you, like William White,
Will quit the club, and never meet with it another night;
You cannot think how many tears your absence brought to me,
And how I've wondered oft and said—what can the matter be?"

JOHN:
"I see it all—no more, Jane, we both were in the wrong;
You scolded me, and I was oft away at night too long.
The bargain close—we must both try henceforward to amend;
When people ask what caused the change, we'll say, the 'Woman's Friend.'"

E. E. CONKLIN & CO.

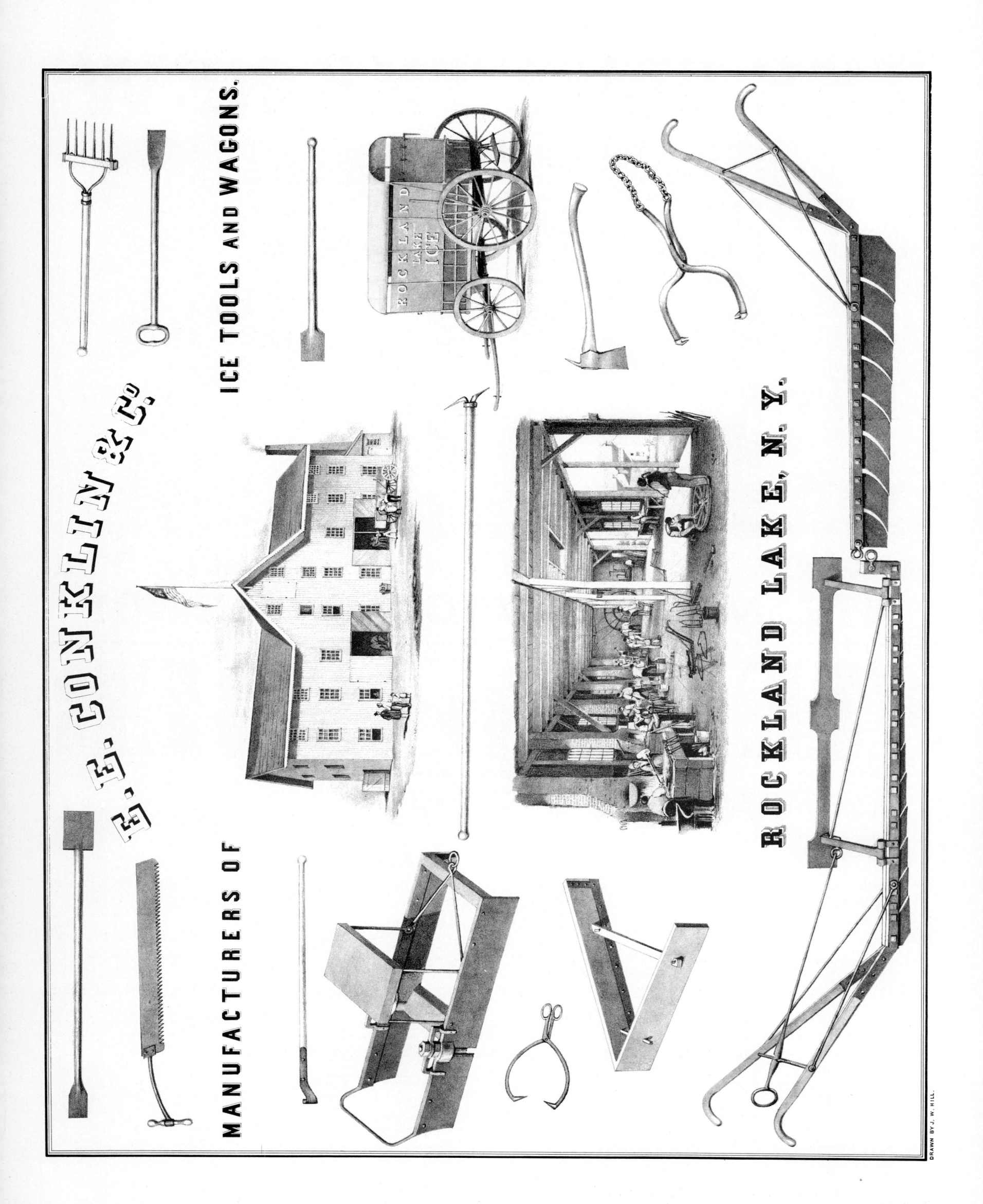

MANUFACTURERS OF ICE TOOLS AND WAGONS.

ROCKLAND LAKE, N. Y.

DRAWN BY J. W. HILL.

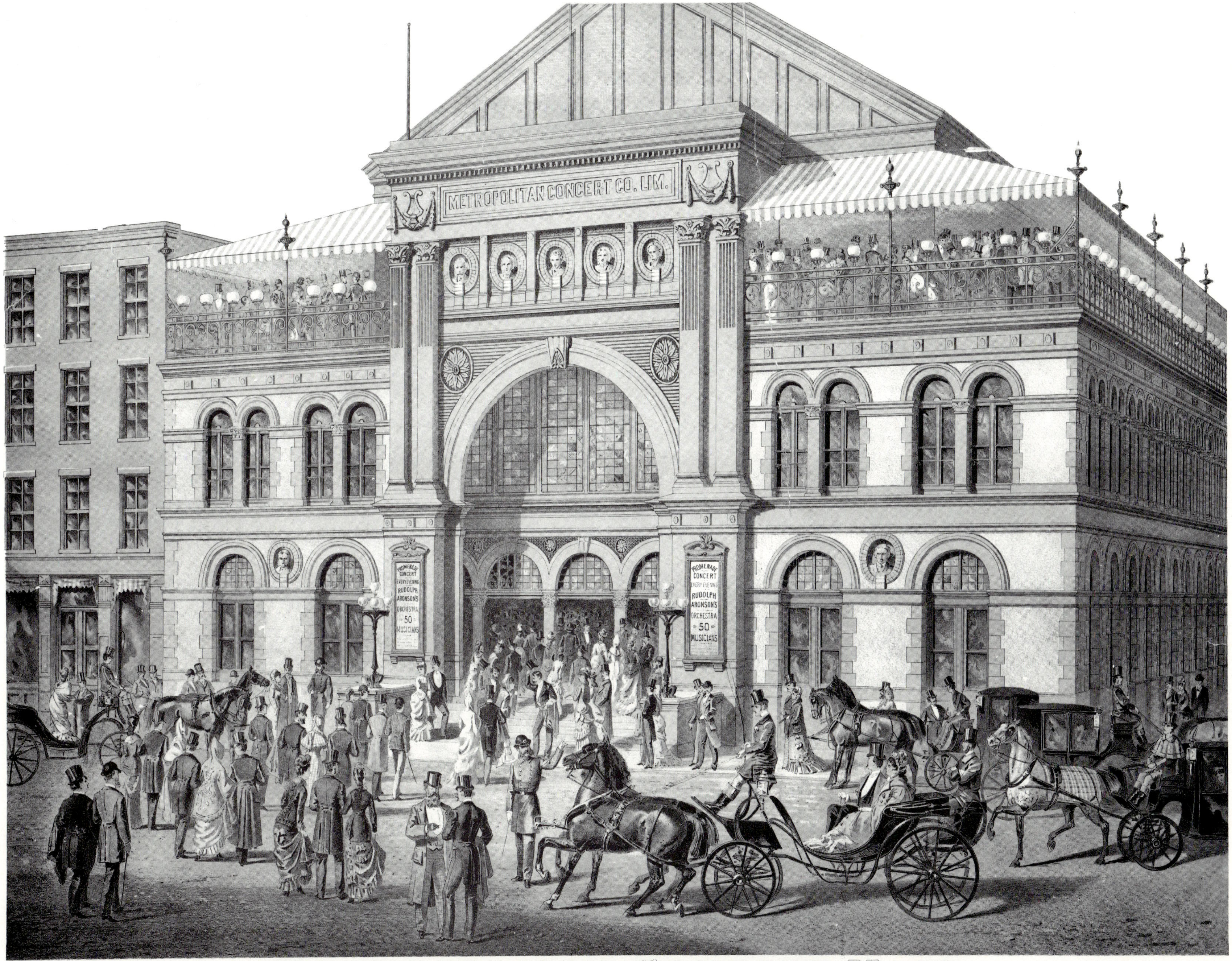

METROPOLITAN CONCERT HALL
BROADWAY, 41ST ST. & 7TH AVENUE N.Y.

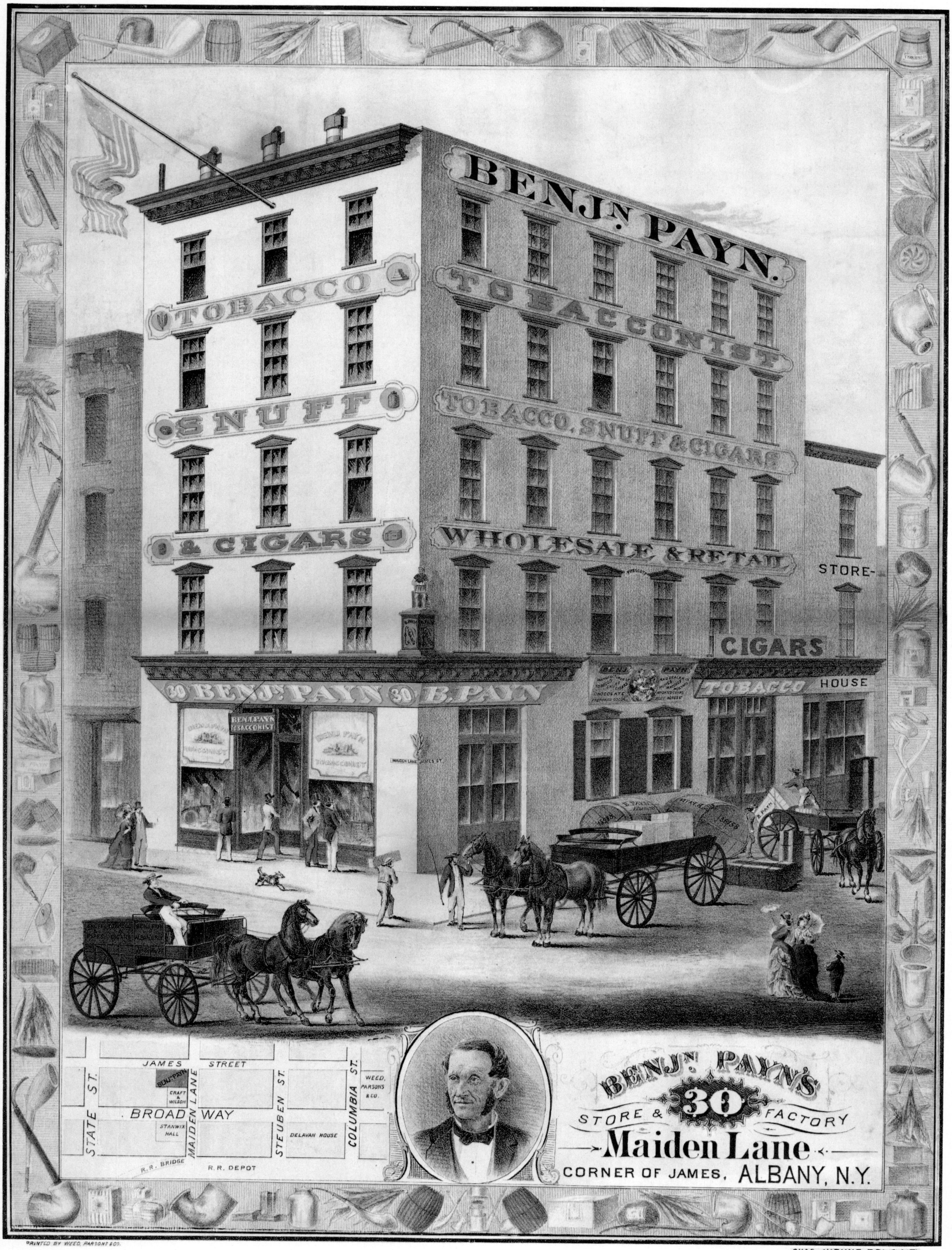

PRINTED BY WEED, PARSONS & CO.

CHAS. JUEHNE DEL. & LITH.

TYLER
PATENT BATTING
WOVEN GAUZE CENTER
14 FEET LONG   3 FEET WIDE
BEST IN THE WORLD

FULL, HONEST WEIGHT.
ONE POUND WILL COVER A LARGE SIZE QUILT AND IS EQUAL TO NEARLY TWO POUNDS MADE IN THE OLD STYLE.
FOR SALE HERE

PATENTED JANUARY 22, 1884.

CABLE SCREW WIRE
BOOTS & SHOES
WILL NOT RIP NOR LEAK

THE
REMINGTON
ARMORY,
AND
SEWING MACHINE WORKS.
ILION, NEW YORK.

G. W. PEABODY'S

Kingston One Price Clothing House.

FINE READY-MADE
CLOTHING!

For Men, Youths', Boys' and Children.

THE BEST GOODS FOR THE LEAST MONEY.

CROSBY BLOCK,

Cor. John & Wall Streets,   KINGSTON, N. Y.

Nugent & Steves, 195 & 197 Fulton Street, N. Y.

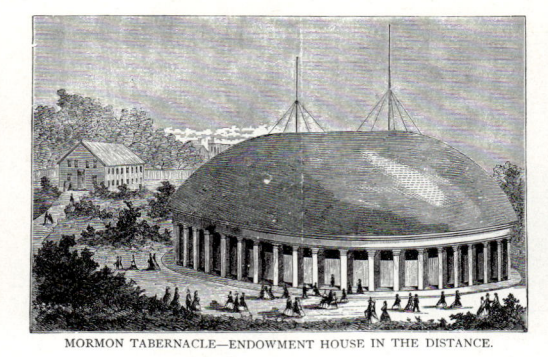

MOUNTAIN MEADOWS MASSACRE—EMIGRANTS KILLED BY MORMONS.   MORMON TABERNACLE—ENDOWMENT HOUSE IN THE DISTANCE.   THE MORMON HAND-CART COMPANY CROSSING THE PLAINS.

POLYGAMY
OR, THE MYSTERIES OF MORMONISM.
BEING AN EXPOSÉ OF THEIR SECRET RITES AND CEREMONIES:

WITH A FULL AND AUTHENTIC HISTORY OF POLYGAMY AND THE MORMON SECT, FROM ITS ORIGIN TO THE PRESENT TIME.

By Hon. O. J. HOLLISTER, U. S. Revenue Collector for Utah.

ILLUSTRATED WITH NEARLY 100 FINE ENGRAVINGS OF LIFE AMONG THE MORMONS.

THE WORK TREATS OF

Mormonism; its origin and history, and shows how, founded on imposture, it has grown by deceit and crime. It shows how Joe Smith was enabled to deceive and cheat his followers; how by leading them on from crime to crime, and enticing them with licentious baits, he succeeded in maintaining his influence over them.

Of the Mormon religion, its infamous and heathenish character, its multitude of gods, its abominable doctrines and practices, revealing many strange mysteries and outrageous ceremonies.

Of the Endowment or initiation ceremonies, showing how obscene and disgusting they are; how female modesty is outraged, and how licentiousness is taught as a part of their religious creed.

Of Polygamy in theory and practice, how it debases society; how it poisons domestic happiness; how it is despised by the women; and how they are forced into it by the Mormon leaders.

Mormonism has been productive of so many dark and strange mysteries—so many terrible crimes that few can comprehend, without an intimate knowledge of it, how much wickedness it has to answer for, and what a standing menace to order and society it is. In this work the author has drawn back the curtain, and has revealed these mysteries and brought to light these crimes, and in doing so, he has presented a work which will startle and horrify every reader.

AGENTS WANTED.—The great desire everywhere manifested to obtain this work, its low price, combined with our very liberal commissions, make this the best chance to make Money ever offered. Agents are meeting with unprecedented success, selling from **FIFTEEN** to **TWENTY** copies per day.

SEND FOR CIRCULARS CONTAINING EXTRA TERMS TO AGENTS, AND A FULL DESCRIPTION OF THE WORK.

ADDRESS, **NATIONAL PUBLISHING CO.**

AT EITHER OF THE FOLLOWING PLACES, WHICHEVER IS NEAREST TO YOU:

Being the most extensive Subscription Book Publishers in the United States, and having four houses, we can afford to sell books cheaper, and pay agents more liberal commissions than any other Company.

728 Cherry St., Philadelphia, Pa.
130 East Adams St., Chicago, Ill.
420 Market St., St. Louis, Mo.
30 So. Broad St., Atlanta, Ga.

SCENES IN THE ENDOWMENT CEREMONIES. 1. Preparation—Washing and Anointing. 2. Enlohim Cursing Adam and Eve—Satan Driven out. 3. Trial of Faith:—"The Searching Hand." 4. Oath to Avenge the Death of Joseph Smith. 5. The "Blood Atonement."

ONLY PART OF A MORMON'S CROP.

JEALOUSY—ONE WIFE TOO MANY.   DR. BENNETT TEACHING THE "SPIRITUAL WIFE" DOCTRINE.   BRIGHAM YOUNG'S DAUGHTER

THE OLD WIFE GETS THE JEWELRY SENT TO THE YOUNG ONE.   "POLYGAMY CRUSHED HER YOUNG HEART."   "I MUST SPEND THE EVENING WITH MY OTHER WIFE."   MORMON'S WIFE HEARING HER HUSBAND HAS TAKEN ANOTHER.

PLEASE POST THIS UP IN A CONSPICUOUS PLACE.

THE STILL ALARM
BY JOSEPH ARTHUR
"Dad's on Fire"
LACY & ARTHUR PROPS & MANAGERS
CENTRAL LITHO. ENG. CO. N.Y.
No 674

DANIEL ROCHAT
THE BETROTHAL
THE MARRIAGE
DIVORCED.
"IT IS DONE"
THE HATCH LITH. CO. 32 & 34 VESEY ST. N.Y.
UNION SQUARE THEATRE
EVERY NIGHT & SATURDAY MATINEE.

GRAND OPERA HOUSE COMMENCING MONDAY, DEC. 4
Saturday Matinees Only.

FORBES CO. BOSTON.

Lotta.

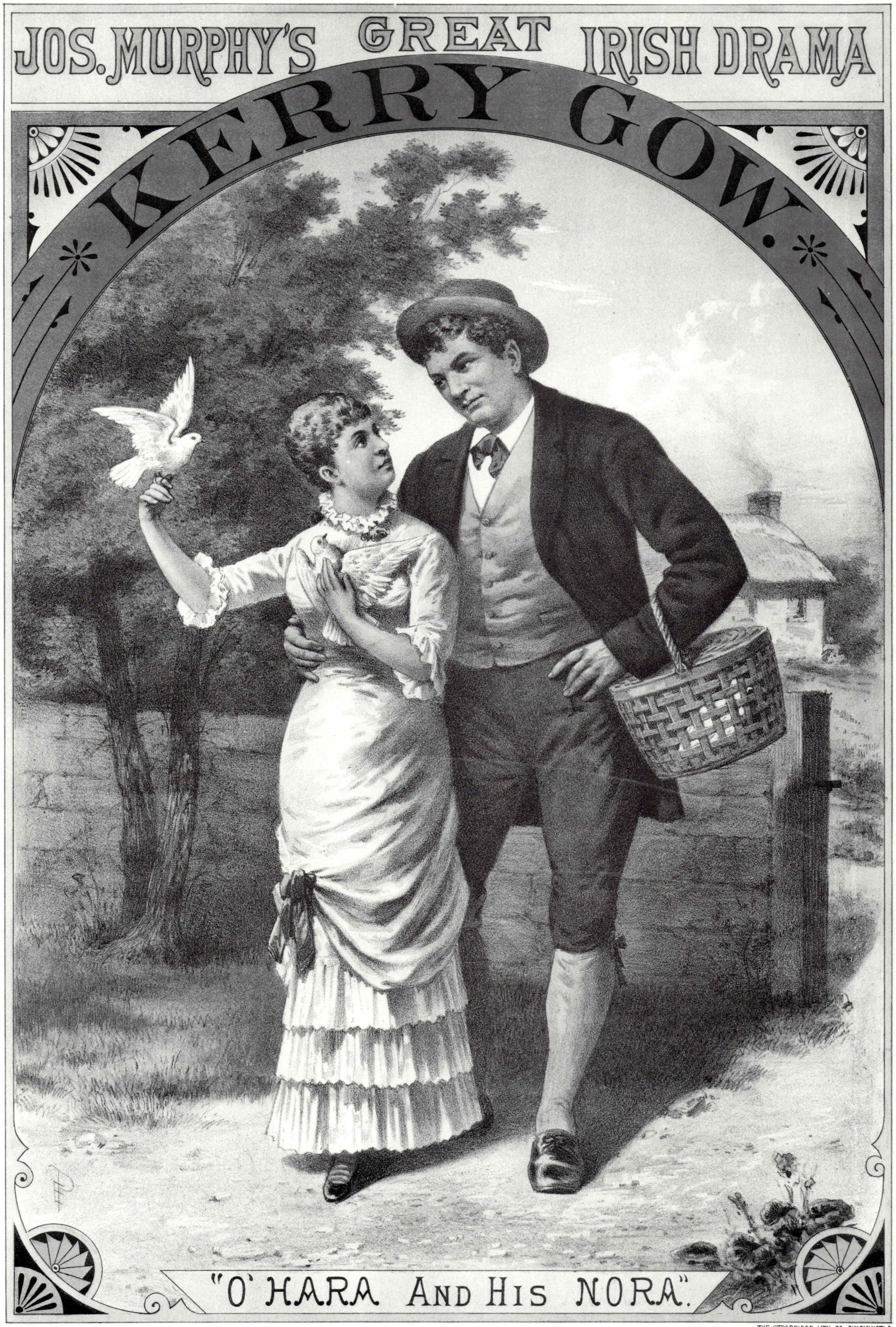

THE STROBRIDGE LITH. CO. CINCINNATI, O.

HAVERLY'S.
BARTLEY CAMPBELL'S
SIBERIA
A NIHILIST.
COMMENCING MONDAY, FEB. 26

W. M. DAVENE'S
ALLIED
ATTRACTIONS
CAPITOLA FORREST
THE CELEBRATED
VOCALIST AND SKIPPING ROPE DANCER
THE STROBRIDGE LITH. CO.
CIN. AND N.Y.
E. Roe
'83

SPECIMEN COPY
CURRIER & IVES'
Illuminated Pictorial Posters
30x42

PACING FOR A GRAND PURSE.

SQUARE WORKS

CHISEL & STEEL

SHAFTSBURY, VERMONT.

THOMAS DOUGLASS, 83 BEEKMAN ST. N.Y.

MANUFACTURER OF SQUARES, CHISELS, SAWS, AXES, HATCHETS, AUGERS, BITTS &c. &c.

Importer and general Dealer in Foreign and Domestic Hardware.

JESSE JAMES COMBINATION

$100,000 REWARD FOR THE CAPTURE OF

JESSE JAMES.

JESSE JAMES.

WINDSOR THEATRE
ONE WEEK, COMMENCING
Monday, Feb. 5
MATINEES WEDNESDAY and SATURDAY.

PROF. D.M. BRISTOL'S EQUESCURRICULUM

PROF. D.M. BRISTOL

HORSE LAUGHING

THE HORSES GOING UP AND DOWN STAIRS

JOHNNIE SANBOURN IN HIS MARVELOUS SWINGING ACT

AT THE BLACK BOARD

POTOSKIE BLACKING THE PROFESSORS BOOTS.

THE COURIER LITH. CO. BUFFALO, N.Y.

ATKINSON COMEDY CO.
IN
PECK'S BAD BOY
·UNDER·THE·MANAGEMENT·OF·
FRED P. WILSON.
LITHO·CO.
N·Y.
THE
CORNER GROCERMAN
AND YOU KNOW THE REST.

MESTAYER-VAUGHN-CO-

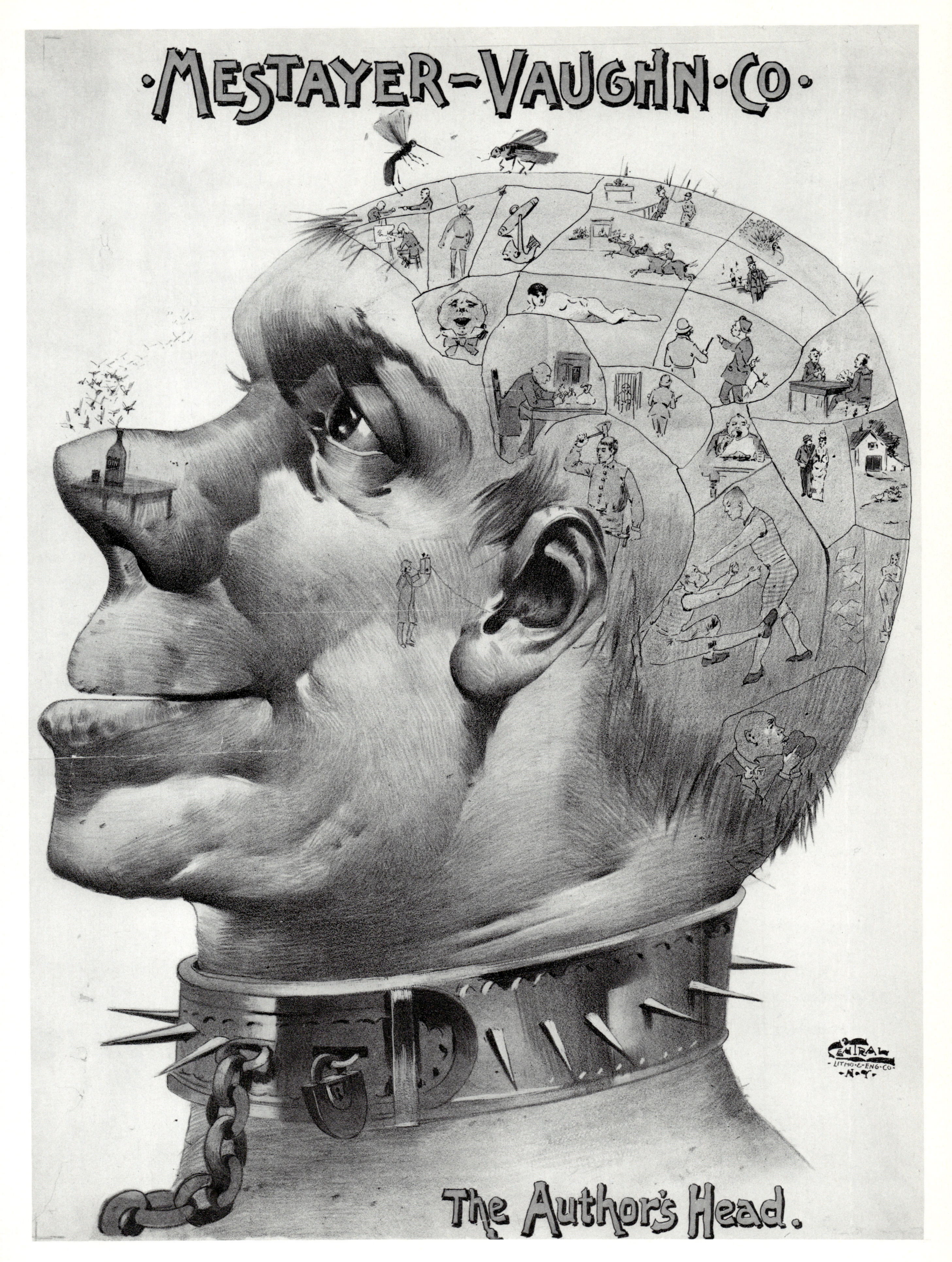

The Author's Head.

SPONGE FISHING.

1 Man that manages the vessel with oars.
2 Men supplying the diver No. 1 with air.
3 Man holding the signal rope.
4 Man in diving dress.
5 Man managing small boat.
6 Man getting sponges with a staff.
7 Man looking through water glass.
8 Man resting himself to dive.
9 Man holding rope for No. 10 to dive.
10 Man diving after No. 14.
11 Man holding rope for No. 15.
12 Man helping No. 13 to get in the vessel.
13 Man getting in vessel.
14 He lost his senses and fell back and was drowned.
15 A man tries to pull out by the roots a big sponge.
16 He signals for the man in the boat to pull him up.
17 A man dressing.
18 Holding rope for No. 23.
19 Pulling up No. 25.
20 Pulling up No. 25.
21 Fixing rope to dive.
22 Lost the rope and tries to get up by himself.
23 Man diving with a rock in his hand.
24 A man tries to pull a sponge out by the roots.
25 A man being drawn up by the rope.
26 Sitting in the shade.
27, 28 Two men taking the drag rope to the head of the boat to pull up.
29 He holds a rock in his hand, ready to dive.
30 Holding the rope for No. 29.
31 Catching No. 32 by the hair as he comes up from diving.
32 He has just gotten up from diving.
33 Helping No. 32 to get in the boat.
34 A man coming up from diving.
35 Is trying to get away from shark.
36 A man destroyed by a shark.
37 Man managing small boat.
38 Waiting to help No. 39 with staff.
39 Man getting sponges with a staff and looking through water glass.
40 Men pulling up the anchor.
41 Man undressing to dive.
42 Men taking out the oars.
43 Man that steers the vessel.
44 Sponge drag.
45 Net bag for man in diving dress to put sponges in.
46 White marble rock, the divers use in diving, weighing 40 lbs., to carry them down quickly.
47 Net bag to put sponges in.

GEO. H. ADAMS'

ADAM FOREPAUGH MANAGER.

GEO. H. ADAMS, CLOWN.

NEW HUMPTY DUMPTY TROUPE.

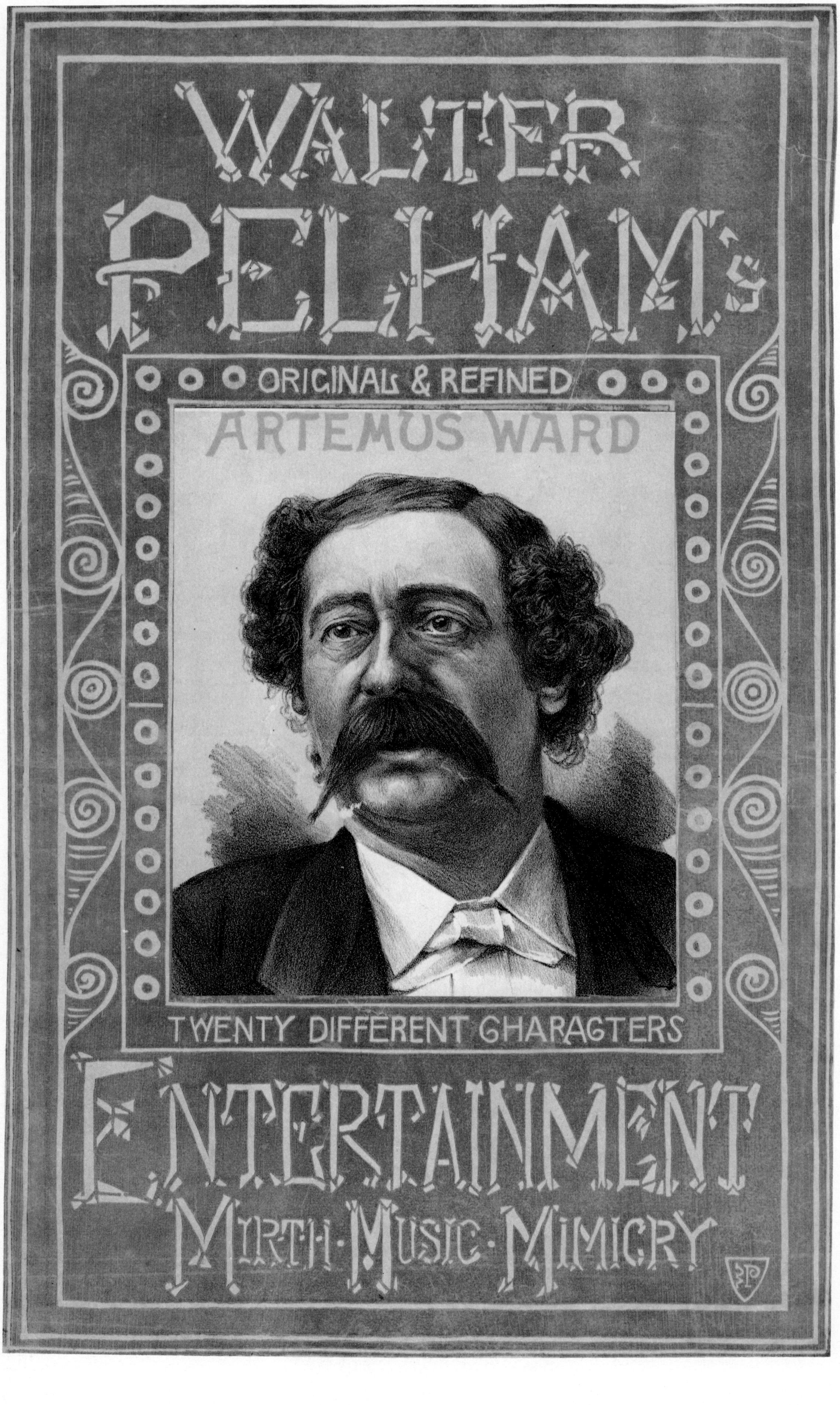
WALTER
PELHAM'S
ORIGINAL & REFINED
ARTEMUS WARD
TWENTY DIFFERENT CHARACTERS
ENTERTAINMENT
MIRTH · MUSIC · MIMICRY

PETTS & STRAFFIN'S
MINSTRELS
CO.
BURLESQUE OPERA TROUPE
W. J. MORGAN & Co LITH. CLEVELAND.O.

THE MOST DELIGHTFUL ROUTE TO THE SEA SHORE
FROM NEW YORK AND NEWARK BY STEAMBOAT TO LOCUST GROVE
STEAM CARS FROM THE GROVE TO CONEY ISLAND
LOCUST GROVE
Schell & Hogan
VIEW FROM LOCUST GROVE PAVILION
OVER THE SALT MEADOWS BY THE BROOKLYN, BATH & CONEY ISLAND R.R.
LITH. OF CHAS. HART 36 VESEY ST. N.Y
IN THE SURF AT CONEY ISLAND
VIEW OF GRAVESEND BAY FROM LOCUST GROVE HOTEL

THE NEW YORK TIMES

SUNDAY, FEB. 9

32 PAGES OF GOOD READING, INCLUDING:

QUEER NATIONAL FIGURES
How Some Statesmen Look to Our Artist. Peculiarities, in Black and White, of Peffer, Jones, Cockrell, Pugh, and Others.

CLARA BARTON'S OLD HOME
The Founder of the Red Cross Society Born in Oxford, Mass. School Teacher and Factory Girl.

MANNING VERSUS NEWMAN
New Light on the Famous Quarrel Between These Celebrated English Prelates.

LOCAL HAUNTS OF AARON BURR
The Home of His Active Years in New-York City. His Marriage to Mme. Jumel and Its Consequences.

COLONIAL NEW-YORK CITY
How Our Ancestors Built a Giant. Thought They'd Found Witches. How Freemasons Were First Regarded.

GENEALOGY OF POKER
All About the Great American Game. It Dates Back a Couple of Centuries.

AMERICA'S FIRST RAILROAD
Ups and Downs in the Development of the Baltimore and Ohio. THE TIMES'S Great "Beat" in 1887.

A MUSEUM OF RELIGIONS
Valuable Collection Recently Mounted at the Smithsonian Institution. Modes of Worship Illustrated.

MANY OTHER FEATURES EQUALLY GOOD. All About Bicycling, Amateur Sports, Art, Society, Drama, Music, and New Literature.

Notes to the Plates

The chronological sequence of the posters is occasionally interrupted in order to effect more visually pleasing or more meaningful combinations. (For technical reasons all the color plates are grouped together before the black-and-white sequence resumes.) The Chronological Index of Posters at the end of the book indicates their exact ordering in time. The Index of Advertisers and the Index of Artists, Engravers, Lithographers, Printers and Publishers, both alphabetical, contain further information on the addresses of the various firms. In the following notes, the numbers that precede the titles of the poster are those of the pages on which the posters are illustrated. The dimensions given (in inches, height before width) are those of the printed areas of the posters, disregarding margins (this type of indication was made necessary by the incompleteness of the edges in numerous cases).

*Inside front cover: CINCINNATI,
HAMILTON & DAYTON R.R.
Lithographer: Strobridge Lithographing Co.,
Cincinnati, 1894. 21⅞ x 13⅛.*

Five or six advertisers, excluding the lithographer, piggyback on the Cincinnati, Hamilton & Dayton train ride. In a city history of the same year, the nearly fifty-year-old line is praised for having the "latest improvements of railroad passenger service," including "Pullman's perfected perpetual safety vestibules." The admirable car pictured is likely to be one of the compartment cars so advertised.

The train is portrayed 25 miles north of Cincinnati as it passes the plant of the Mosler Safe Co. in Hamilton, in adjoining Butler County. Imported across the Indiana state line is Aurora Export Beer, while Cincinnati's own storekeeper, the Joseph R. Peebles Sons Co. (established 1840), supplies both Cabinet Whiskey and Peebles Perfectos. One of the city's great industries is represented in the advertisement of the Cook Carriage Co.; with more than a hundred styles of two and four-wheelers to choose from, it was one of the largest makers of four to fifteen-passenger vehicles in the world. This civic boast is published in the pages of one of the local papers, *The Cincinnati Times-Star*.

The Strobridge Co. is best known for its theatrical posters, a number of which are included in the present collection.

*Inside back cover, left: J. & P. COATS.
1885. 28½ x 13.*

*Right: J. & P. COATS BEST SIX-CORD
SPOOL COTTON.
About 1890. 27⅞ x 11¾.*

Far-flung East Coast locations for the production of J. & P. Coats six-ply thread are brought close in the interesting 1885 poster on the left; the all-important end product is illustrated in a central lozenge.

Coats & Clark (the company created in 1952 from J. & P. Coats and the slightly earlier firm of James and Patrick Clark) has identified two of the scenes from a copyrighted print of the same poster in its collection. The view at the top is a Sea Island cotton field. At the lower left, one of the company's American factories is illustrated, the J. & P. Coats Thread Works in Pawtucket, Rhode Island, purchased during the Civil War from Samuel Conant, Jr. The new plant was acquired in 1864 as the firm encountered difficulty in importing American cotton to Paisley, Scotland, the headquarters of its founder, James Coats. The dock scene is unidentified, but it may represent the loading of cotton bales in Georgia for transportation by freighter to the Rhode Island plant.

As a result of the invention of the sewing machine, George Clark, the rival of the Coats firm, developed a strong thread suitable for the new machine. In the poster from about 1890 the Coats Co. advertises a similar six-cord thread, and crows that its product is "best" for hand and machine. The poster emphasizes its strength as the pug pulls J. & P. Coats thread from a spool in another of the opulent Victorian interiors that poster artists delighted in presenting.

*Frontispiece: SILVER TIP SHOES.
Artist: J. [probably James A.] Shearman.
Lithographer: Peter Calvi. Printers: Major &
Knapp Engraving, Manufacturing & Lithographing Co., New York, about 1880.
18¾ x 14⅜.*

Aside from its advertising message, this cheerful domestic scene in an elegant Victorian parlor might be a scene from *Life with Father* by Howard Lindsay and Russell Crouse. The high-ceilinged paneled room, with puffy button-tufted chairs and figured carpet, provides a high-style setting for demonstration of the useful qualities of Silver Tip Shoes. In contrast to the metal-tipped protection offered, but barely visible on the new high-button shoes, the angelic children left and center display the disadvantages of the regular sort of untipped shoes. The maker of the shoes is not identified in New York directories, although it would be pleasant to think that George and David Silver, in "shoes" at 18 Warren Street, might be the manufacturers.

*1. FIRTH, HALL & POND.
New York, about 1842. 10⅞ x 7⅞.*

This charming small poster is the earliest one illustrated in this book. It exhibits the exuberant high style of New York furniture of the late Empire period, in which pillar and scroll were the most noticeable design features. Both the pianoforte and stool are good examples of this period of cabinetmaking. The fashionably dressed piano player and elaborate window drapery, with fringed valance artfully draped over an arrow-shaped rod, complete the effect.

John Firth and William Hall, musical-instrument makers, established a pianoforte and music warehouse at 1 Franklin Square in the 1830s. In the early 1840s Silvanus B. Pond joined the organization. The firm was also one of the major nineteenth-century publishers of American popular songs, including works by Stephen Foster.

2. THE NEW YORK SCIENTIFIC AMERICAN.
Publisher: Scientific American, New York, about 1845. 21⅞ x 17½.

Since Rufus Porter, the founder of *Scientific American*, is listed as editor on this attractive poster with wood-engraved illustrations, it must have been published during the newspaper's first year. Early in 1846 Porter departed, selling the paper to Orson Munn and Alfred E. Beach. Beach was publisher and co-owner of the *New York Sun*, then located in the building at the corner of Fulton and Nassau Streets, where the *Scientific American* also had its offices. Besides being a publisher and editor, Porter was a fiddler, drummer, painter and inventor. His many talents were those of a jack-of-all-trades although he was master of many of them.

Rufus Porter was born in Boxford, Massachusetts. At the age of fifteen he became a shoemaker's apprentice but he soon left his bench for fiddle and fife, playing these instruments for a military company and for dancing parties in Portland, Maine. At eighteen he was apprenticed to a house painter, a profession he put to use in the War of 1812 when he painted gunboats. At the same time he continued to play the fife in the Portland Light Infantry. Among the occupations he pursued for stints of various duration before briefly coming to rest in New York were school teaching, windmill construction and the invention of a camera obscura as an aid to portrait painting.

In 1823 he was in Hartford with designs for a twin boat propelled by horsepower, and in 1824 he began to paint freehand landscape murals in houses, inns and public buildings. Much of his fame, now as then, rests on these large wall decorations.

3. SAMUEL C. JOLLIE & CO.
Wood engraver: George W. Teubner, New York, about 1845. 11¼ x 7¼.

One of the small gems of the Landauer Collection is this early black-and-white poster that provides an informative mid-century view of three beautiful Federal houses on Broadway "near White-street, N. Y."

In the late 1830s, Samuel C. Jollie bought out William Millet's interest in the musical-instrument firm of Jollie and Millet, which had been located in the building shown here. Millet set up a similar business a little south of Jollie's Broadway store. In 1845, the approximate date of the Teubner engraving, Allen R. and Edward Jollie are listed in the New York directory as musical-instrument makers at 66 Walker Street. Since all three Jollies then lived at 459 Greenwich Avenue, it may be supposed that the "Superior Toned Flutes" and "Flageolets, Clarionets and Fifes" being advertised were of Jollie family manufacture.

The William Boyd "Confectionary" moved from Front Street to the beautiful storefront residence shown here about 1839. Anna and J. and E. Whittingham purveyed French millinery as well as fancy goods from the slightly smaller house to the right. Teubner, whose name appears below the Jollie shop window, lived on East Broadway in the 1840s. He may have worked for Samuel Jollie in engraving and printing, "with the utmost neatness," the professional and visiting cards advertised at the bottom of the poster.

4. PAYN & McNAUGHTON; TOBACCO.
Probably Albany, about 1847. 22 x 19½.

Undoubtedly the seven tobacco users in the central vignette, whose visages are repeated on labels for Payn & McNaughton's "Extra Fine Cut James River Cavendish" and elsewhere, are the figures represented on the "Sign of Seven Heads" that the Albany directory tells us marked the Payn & McNaughton store after 1846. The scents of chocolate and tobacco intermingled in the shop must have been an invitation to turn in at the sign. The quality of the firm's products was established by award of the "Highest Premium from the New-York State Agricultural Society," providing yet another reason to use its Cavendish, Rose Scented Maccoboy, Extra Fine Yellow Banks Kentucky Chewing Tobacco and Pure Ground Chocolate and Prepared Cocoa.

Payn & McNaughton are first listed at the 7 Broadway address given here in 1846; this poster must predate 1852, when Broadway street numbers were changed and number 7 became 477. The neighboring E. Corning and Co. referred to was Erastus Corning's hardware store. Corning, who had been mayor of Albany and later went into railroads, was the great-grandfather of Erastus Corning II, the present mayor. For another Payn poster, see page 72.

5. NEW LINE BETWEEN ALBANY & NEWBURG.
Probably Albany, 1849. 13⅜ x 8⅝.

This handsome poster clearly shows the graining of the wood type used to announce the *St. Nicholas* as the vessel inaugurating the thrice-weekly run between Newburgh and Albany, stopping at large and small Hudson River landings along the way. The flag depicted in the woodcut of the twin-stacked, walking-beam side-wheeler originally bore the name *Santa Klaus*. The words are scratched through as though the owners had elected the saintly Christmas figure as their symbol, rather than the one celebrated by Washington Irving. Two pilothouse figures, an eagle and a runner with bow and arrow, suggest the possibility of an earlier, different designation for this vessel. Passengers and cabins occupy the after end, while freight is sheltered under a canopy forward.

6. BARNUM'S AMERICAN MUSEUM.
Artists & lithographers: Eliphalet Brown, Jr., & Charles Severin. Printer: G. W. Lewis, New York, 1851–52. 22¼ x 29⅜.

A print of this fabulous view of Barnum's American Museum was sold at auction in Northampton, Massachusetts, in 1920 as part of Tom Thumb's effects, a prized possession, no doubt, of this most famous of P. T. Barnum's entertainers.

Barnum presented Jenny Lind in her American debut at Castle Garden, September 5, 1850. Tickets for this concert were sold at auction, and Barnum's friend and neighbor, the hatter Genin (whose shop is shown to the right of the American Museum), bought the first ticket at $225. That action, which brought him both notoriety and increased business, was undoubtedly the basis for the Jenny Lind riding hats he advertises here. The five-story building, on the corner of Ann Street and Broadway, was convenient to City Hall, the Astor House and St. Paul's Chapel in the busiest section of the city —Barnum's contribution to the activity in this area being no small one. In 1849 he expanded his museum to include a theatre; the following year, he enlarged the theatre to seat 3000.

Many of Barnum's other neighbors are named in this exciting poster. Included among them are a soda-water manufacturer, the only papier-mâché warehouse in America, the publishers of the *International Magazine*, J. A. Walnut's "Live and Let Live" Oyster Saloon and the New York Surgeons Bandage Institute.

The designers of the poster were the Danish artist Charles Severin and Eliphalet Brown, Jr. The latter, best known for a series of views of Perry's Japan expedition executed in 1856, was also the creator of the poster on page 7.

7. THE AUTOMATODEON.
Artist & lithographer: Eliphalet Brown, Jr.
Printer: James Ackerman, New York, 1850.
24 x 33¾.

This picture of an exotic procession in sight of Castle Garden and the Battery was printed by the firm of James Ackerman at 379 Broadway, one of its several lower-Manhattan locations. The designs drawn on the elaborate chariot (possibly housing a steam calliope or an organ) hint at the wonders of the G. C. Quick menagerie carried in the sedate wagons shown in the middle ground. Hidden within are American panthers, spotted hyenas, royal Bengal and "Brazillian" tigers, a polar bear, an Asiatic lion and lioness and African leopards. The caparisoned camels led by Bolivar, the Asiatic elephant, were undoubtedly a tantalizing suggestion of mysterious creatures yet to be seen.

8. JOSEPH LAING & CO.; EDWARD EVANS.
Lithographer: Joseph Laing & Co., New York,
about 1854. 19½ x 15¼.

Surrounded by muses of poetry, art, music and science, the mercantile houses of Edward Evans and Joseph Laing, at the southeast corner of Fulton Street and Ryders Alley, provide the center of interest in this double advertisement for firms sharing a single building. The arms of New York and the shield of the United States are symbolic of the kind of printing that provided Laing with a great part of his business: the company specialized in the beautiful county and city bank notes and bills of exchange on tissue-thin paper that were common until the establishment of a third national bank and a national system of paper money in 1864.

The Washington Monument shown here is one of the elaborate projected designs; the actual structure (not dedicated until 1885, although the cornerstone was laid on July 4, 1848) was much simplified. This poster therefore dates from about 1854, a year consistent with the carriage, horsecar and wagon illustrated in this busy scene at 66 Fulton Street in New York City.

9. BABY JUMPER. OR TUTTLE'S PATENT INFANT GYMNASIUM.
Lithographer: W. J. Dailey, probably London
(New Cut, Lambeth), about 1850. 20½ x 15.

The title block and the fringed draperies that fall from it make a proscenium arch for this charming illustration for George W. Tuttle's Patent Infant Gymnasium, manufactured and distributed from a narrow third-class building on the west side of Broadway that looked out onto the grounds of New York Hospital.

The baby jumper was constructed from strong elastic, and ended in a harness to hold the child, permitting it to exercise in a manner that must have looked like a chandelier in motion. All appears to be right in the world for the participants in this domestic scene: happy baby, fond parents and attentive nurse. The toys—soft knitted ball, punch-on-a-stick and wicker rattle—are characteristic of babies' playthings of this period.

10. CONGRESS STOVE POLISH.
Lithographers: James A. Shearman & Charles
H. Hart, New York, about 1861. 18⅛ x 12½.

Mayhem in the parlor is the theme of this scene, one of a long and curious catalog of dramatic incidents created by commercial illustrators. The manufacturers of this obviously useful polish-of-more-than-one-purpose cannot be located in New York directories, but the two lithographers are listed together at a Fulton Street location only from 1861 to 1863.

Anyone who has ever used a kitchen or parlor wood or coal stove knows the pleasures of a superior polish; the smell and the emerging black patent shine of the stove are satisfactions hard to beat. Even as the older children raise Cain, the youngest already understands the delight of a gleaming stove as she works away at her miniature kitchen range.

11. MRS. S. A. ALLEN'S WORLD'S HAIR RESTORER.
Lithographers: Napoleon Sarony, Richard
Major & Joseph F. Knapp, New York,
about 1860. 19⅛ x 15½.

Most likely to have been the producer and purveyor of "World's Hair-Restorer" and "World's Hair-Dressing or Zylobalsamum" is Susan Allen, a perfumer at 355 Broome Street in Manhattan. Perfumers commonly sold cosmetics, hair dye and restorer as well as other beauty preparations. Despite the promise to mend "the bald & the grey," the portraits of woman and girl reflected in a mirror suggest eternal beauty and youth with little need for the miracle promised in the text.

The poster, surrounded by a strapwork border, is the work of Sarony, Major & Knapp, lithographers at 449 Broadway, where "a large corps of talented artists and printers enables us to produce every variety of work with dispatch." They did commercial work of every description, operating forty lithographic presses in the back room on the first of three floors in a large building 25 by 200 feet. The trio were in business together from about 1857 to 1864. Prospective customers were invited to visit the "Practical Lithographers'" business office and specimen room on the first floor at the entrance to the building. Sarony is also remembered as one of the great New York portrait photographers of the nineteenth century.

12. HENRY MILLER'S TOBACCO.
Lithographers: Napoleon Sarony & Richard
Major, New York, about 1855. 24 x 18.

Henry Miller's "gorgeous tobacco chariot" passes along Broadway opposite the St. Nicholas Hotel just four years after its construction. The builder, G. H. Haight, named the hotel for the St. Nicholas Society, of which he was a member. It was demolished in 1864, but was described in Francis' 1854 *New Guide to the Cities of New-York and Brooklyn:*

> No establishment of the kind in New-York and perhaps none in the world, can surpass the elegance of the St. Nicholas. Its front of white marble, extending 300 feet on Broadway, near Spring street, is a conspicuous object; while the whole interior with its spacious halls, and its wonderful profusion of mirrors, (numbering 110), increases the admiration of the visitor. The cost of the completed building and its furniture is not far from $1,000,000. The hotel consists, in fact, of three structures . . . which together are capable of affording room for about 1000 guests. The cooking apparatus and the laundry are very complete, and may be seen without inconvenience. The great attraction, however, is the bridal chamber—a dazzling apartment, hung with white satin, and with exception of its gas fixtures, probably the most elegant and sumptuous room in New-York. We are not aware of the price set upon entertainment in such style, but

NOTES TO THE PLATES

presume that the cost of a honeymoon in this glittering dormitory would suffice to support a quiet couple for some years.

In this period Sarony and Major were in business together before Knapp joined the partnership.

13. RESOLUTE FIRE INSURANCE COMPANY OF THE CITY OF NEW YORK.
Lithographer: Hatch & Co., New York, about 1863. 22⅛ x 17¼.

In 1863, the firm of Hatch & Co. reprinted this poster from one published in 1861 by James A. Shearman and Charles H. Hart, the designers of this charming little stage on which a banner bearing the mid-century design for the arms of New York is displayed. The sailor and Indian are later versions of earlier supporters of the New York shield, on which appear the traditional symbols representing the sources of the economy of the New York Province and the company-governed town of the Dutch West India Company. The windmill arms, beaver and flour barrel are augmented here by anchor, quadrant and brass gun barrel.

Directors of the Resolute Fire and Inland Navigation Co. are listed in ribbons of type spiraling up the pillar supports, the base inscribed with the names of William D. Randell, the company secretary, and John E. Uhlhorn, its president.

14. LOVE TOBACCO.
Lithographer: Calvert Lithographing and Engraving Co., Detroit, about 1867. 25⅝ x 19½.

Advertisements for tobacco offer a wide variety of images; this unusual scene appears to illustrate the name of the chewing tobacco. A plug of Love is offered to a Northern scout in blue by a Southern soldier in gray. It seems likely that this is a retrospective view of the War Between the States, and one that would hardly have been published while the Civil War was in progress. This theory is supported by the Southern location of the Myers Brothers' factory, while the manufacturer of the poster had his plant in Detroit. The Calvert Co. was established in 1861 and incorporated in 1867; its full-color, embossed advertisements in Detroit directories suggest designs that would have been especially appropriate for cigar bands and boxes and for chewing-tobacco labels; it may have been this capability that first brought it to the attention of the Richmond firm.

15. NIAGARA LEAP BY THE WONDERFUL BUISLAY FAMILY.
Lithographer: Charles H. Hart, New York, 1866. 22⅞ x 18⅛.

Near the end of the last regular season at the New Bowery Theatre on The Bowery between Canal and Hester Streets, the house was taken over by the remarkable family of aerialists and gymnasts pictured here. Buislay family members included Etienne, Adolphe, Julio, Grenet, Justin, Master Joaquin and Mlle. Luisa. Before coming to New York they had performed in Paris, where they had introduced a new burlesque, "Le Pied du Mouton," which they included in their bill for the 1865–66 season in New York. On June 16 they opened at the New Bowery to favorable critical notices and remained there until late July. The Niagara Leap was the hit of the show; the most talented Buislay aerialist—pictured as a giant dragonfly in mid-flight—appears to swing from lines in the theatre auditorium, flying over orchestra and stage apron, past balcony tiers and boxes, toward a backdrop painted to resemble the great Falls and its rainbow. The next season at the New Bowery was its last. The theatre was destroyed on December 18, 1866, in the fourth major theatre fire in New York since the middle of 1865.

16. PATENT CYLINDER LITHOGRAPHIC PRINTING MACHINE.
Lithographers: Forst, Averell & Co., New York, about 1870. 17 x 22.

This poster featuring the rotary press of R. Hoe & Co. shows one of the machines that revolutionized printing in America from the 1850s to the 1880s, permitting production of almost six times the number of impressions that were possible by flat-bed press and making the modern newspaper possible. Richard M. Hoe, son of Robert Hoe, founder of the firm, invented the rotary cylinder press in London in 1846; in the 1870s the Hoe company still maintained a shop there.

In the period of this advertisement Peter S., Richard M., Robert II and Robert III Hoe, were all engaged in the family's press and saw-manufacturing business in New York. Their machine and press shop and their steam-engine plant occupied a large part of the block bounded by Broome, Sheriff, Columbia and Gold Streets; their warehouse was located at the northeast corner of Platt and Gold Streets. The poster was printed by the New York firm of Forst and Averell, engravers, lithographers, label manufacturers and letterpress printers at 28 Platt Street, near the Hoe plant.

17. WASON CAR MANUFACTURING CO.
Springfield, Massachusetts (?), 1872. 19⅞ x 30⅜.

The Wason railroad-car manufacturers were located in the Brightwood section in northwest Springfield. The Chicopee River is seen behind the factory, and one of the elegant sleeping and drawing-room cars of the New York-to-Boston run is illustrated. Thomas W. Wason was president of the firm and the vice-president was George C. Fisk, whose name is stenciled on one of the packing crates illustrated. The train to New York and Albany passed by the picturesque Wason plant four times daily and once on Sunday.

18. E. BUTTERICK & CO'S. QUARTERLY REPORT OF NEW YORK FASHIONS.
Lithographer: Hatch Lithographic Co., New York, 1873. 20⅞ x 25⅛.

This fashionable assembly, gathered on the east bank of the Hudson, are holding their sociable conclave in what appears to be the area near Peekskill. Twenty-two figures at an overlook on the Hudson might have observed the steamboats and sailboats plying the river; their chief interest, however, is obviously fashion as the models strike poses in this unlikely location for a Victorian ladies' promenade. The Butterick firm published similar posters four times a year, often with New York scenes to add spice to stylish apparel.

The company was founded by Ebenezer Butterick only fourteen years prior to the date of the poster, when he began to make graded patterns for shirts, an idea initiated by either Butterick or his wife Ellen. The first of the stiff paper patterns appeared on the market in June 1863. That same year, Butterick set up production in Fitchburg, Massachusetts, for pattern manufacture and distribution, and added designs for Garibaldi suits for boys. In 1864 Butterick located on lower Broadway in New York and began to make tissue-paper patterns for children's suits, soon adding women's patterns to his line. The factory was moved from Fitchburg to Brooklyn in 1869, when a magazine of fashion reports was established by Butterick and his associates. Paper patterns caught on like wildfire, with six million sold in 1871. Three years after this "Report" the Butterick firm had its principal office in a narrow five-story building at 555 Broadway and branches in London, Paris, Berlin and Vienna. The firm is still active in the fashion field; since the turn of the century it has occupied its own building at 161 Sixth Avenue (corner of Spring Street).

19. DOMESTIC SEWING MACHINES.
Probably New York, about 1874. 18½ x 24⅝.

In 1874 the Domestic Sewing Machine Co. was listed at three New York locations. The company's store at the southwest corner of 14th Street and Broadway, across from Union Square and in the heart of the fashionable shopping district, is the one shown in the poster. The sewing machine in the window is dwarfed by its opulent setting, but chandeliers cast a strong light on it and the fashionable dresses that illustrate its performance in the hands of a skilled dressmaker.

In the promenade past this busy corner, only a bellboy (extreme right) falls outside the elegance and sophistication of the strolling figures. Most of the walkers seem to know one another, and each of their costumes is a triumph of the arts of tailor or dressmaker.

The Domestic Sewing Machine Co. was established by William A. Mack and N. S. Perkins in Norwalk, Ohio, in 1864. In 1869 it was incorporated, adopting the company name seen here. The firm still exists as a subsidiary of the White Sewing Machine Co. of Cleveland, Ohio, which acquired the older company in 1924.

20. THE "UNCLE SAM" RANGE.
*Lithographers: Schumacher & Louis Ettlinger,
New York, 1876. 13¼ x 20⅜.*

Two years after the exposition at Philadelphia the Abendroth Brothers, Augustus and William, first appeared in the New York Directory at the Beekman and Pearl Street addresses shown here, yet internal evidence in this ambitious unsigned poster indicates that it was published in the nation's centennial year.

Uncle Sam's Little Dinner Party of 1876 was clearly a celebration to remember. "Feeding the World" are Uncle Sam and Columbia, who preside at a banquet table at which the children "Dixie," "West" and "New England" are already seated. The flag-patterned room, with starred and striped carpet, wallpaper and drapery, overlooks the Centennial grounds.

The long bill of fare is international, with offerings of English roast beef, German "Sour Crout," French "Donkey a la Mode," Irish potatoes—fried, boiled, stewed, roasted, baked, mashed and raw—Chinese rats "Fricaseed" with watermelon seeds, Italian roasted sardines, Russian white bear and Turkish pistachio nuts. The American contribution appears to be the turkey roasting in the "Uncle Sam" Range, manufactured by the Abendroths, probably at their foundry located at the foot of East 118th Street.

Of the two lithographers, only Louis Ettlinger is listed in this period, his shop located at 15 Murray Street.

21. COLONEL KANE'S COACH;
*J. B. BREWSTER & CO.
Lithographer: Endicott & Co., New York,
1876. 25½ x 35⅞.*

This poster can only hint at the excitement attendant on the inauguration of a regular coach run out of New York. Colonel De Lancey Kane purchased a tallyho in England and had it shipped to New York in the centennial year. A number of the gentlemen illustrated were founding members of the Coaching Club of New York, formed to introduce road coaching to the American public. Identified enthusiasts in this portrait included F. Bronson (far left) and Colonel and Mrs. De Lancey Kane in the front and driver's seat. The first passenger seat is occupied by W. L. Kane, F. Sherman and Colonel William Jay; the man with the horn is Arthur Fownes, a guard; the man inside the coach is a mechanic from the Brewster Coach and Carriage Co. who went along to do any necessary repairs. Except for Mrs. Kane, the ladies are unidentified and replace three men who appear in the original painting.

In the period of this poster, the distinguished carriage-making firm of J. B. Brewster & Co. (established in 1838) occupied a fine gable-ended factory building at 145 East 25th Street and had "warerooms" on Fifth Avenue (corner of 27th Street). In 1871 the company advertisement included an endorsement from General George B. McClellan; the Civil War general lauded the Brewster Patent Vertical Steel Plate Axle as "two and a half (2½) times" as effective as an ordinary axle.

Twelve Brewster carriages are in the collections of the New-York Historical Society, all but one the 1938 gift of Harris Fahnstock, who, until the late 1930s, maintained and used the Brewster Stanhope Gig, Dogcart, Runabout, Demi-Mail Phaeton, Basket Vis-à-Vis, Caleche and Panel-Boot Victoria as pleasure vehicles at Eastover, his Lenox (Massachusetts) estate.

22. THE GREAT EAST RIVER
SUSPENSION BRIDGE.
*Artists: Charles R. Parsons &
Lyman W. Atwater.
Lithographers: Currier & Ives, New York,
1877. 24¼ x 32⅞.*

The marvel of its age, the suspension bridge across the East River designed by John A. Roebling and completed after his death by his son William A. Roebling (as Chief Engineer), is the center of interest in this busy marine view. The poster was commissioned by the leather and findings company of Mulford, Cary & Conklin, with main offices at 34 Spruce Street, between William and Gold Streets in lower Manhattan.

Details of the bridge's dimensions are given in this poster made six years before the dedication of the Brooklyn Bridge in 1883. Side-wheelers and cargo sailing ships ply the East River, while the pier just south of the Manhattan tower shows bales of calfskins, sheepskins and moroccos intended for Mulford, Cary & Conklin. Noted in the poster is the bridge approach opposite City Hall, just three minutes away from the company's store.

Charles R. Parsons, son of the artist Charles Parsons and nephew of lithographer Charles H. Hart, became associated with Lyman W. Atwater in 1863. The firm was noted for the marine views it created for Currier & Ives and for Endicott & Co.

23. THE ONLY ROUTE VIA NIAGARA
FALLS & SUSPENSION BRIDGE.
*Lithographers: Clay, Cosack & Co.,
Buffalo, 1876. 17¼ x 25⅞.*

A view of the railroad suspension bridge at Niagara Falls on the Great Central Route (New York and Boston westward to Chicago and San Francisco) is incorporated into this dramatic view of the Falls. A "Palace Sleeping Car" passes between the bridge towers, its passengers given an unparalleled view of the Falls as they make their westward progress in a luxurious car with curtained windows. Twenty years before this poster was made, the Great Western Railway described the virtues of sleeping cars on this route: the trains had permanent berths fitted with hair mattresses "resting on Spiral Springs" and offered as "comfortable rest as in any first-class Hotel." In this period, the Michigan Central Railroad operated the Great Central Route via the Falls and bridge; in addition to its sixteen-wheel sleeping cars, the line offered Ruttan's Ventilating Apparatus in all passenger cars and promised "Palace, Hotel and Drawing Room Cars" on through trains between Boston and Chicago.

Immediately left of the central pylon may be seen one of the many interesting commercial buildings that exist in the landscapes and cityscapes pictured in these posters; the structure in the shadow of the bridge is identified as Witmer's Mill.

24. SAM'L OF POSEN, THE COMMERCIAL DRUMMER.
Lithographer: Strobridge Lithographing Co., Cincinnati & New York, 1882. 29¼ x 17¼.

Late in the spring of 1881, *Samuel of Posen* opened with M. B. Curtis in the title of Samuel Plastrick, a characterization that Odell, in his *Annals of the New York Stage*, describes as launching the actor "into stellardom, in a piece that lasted him for years." The story of the Jewish commercial traveler and his high jinks opened at Haverly's 14th Street Theatre in New York on May 16 and lasted until August 6. Several revivals followed and this poster is for one of them: a fortnight's performance at the same theatre during the holiday season of 1882.

25. THE ORIGINAL BLACK CROOK.
Lithographer: Strobridge Lithographing Co., Cincinnati, New York & London, about 1881. 23⅜ x 12⅞.

The first performance of *The Black Crook* took place at Niblo's Garden in New York on September 12, 1866. Five days later an account in the *Tribune* catalogued its wonders and characterized its drama:

" 'The Black Crook' was played by easy stages from 7¾ o'clock until 1¼. Most of the auditors remained until the gorgeous end. . . . The scenery is magnificent; the ballet is beautiful; the drama is — rubbish." The spectacle lasted 475 performances, a record in its time. Its many revivals may be explained in George C. D. Odell's analysis of the play, recorded in his encyclopedic *Annals of the New York Stage*:

> The Black Crook has become a name, a symbol among us. More than fifty years after its original production it [was] still known to youngsters as the bold, daring, unclad ballet show that threatened to lead their grandfathers down what the old preachers called the path to hell. The spectacle remains in popular consciousness as the first attempt to put on the stage the wild delirious joy of a sensualist's fantasy.

The performance of the "original" Black Crook advertised in this poster took place after 1880, the year that Strobridge & Co. became the Strobridge Lithographing Co. Most likely it was the one, at Niblo's Garden again, on March 7, 1881, when Pauline Markham played the part of the subaqueous Queen Stalacta as *The Black Crook* took over the boards for a five-week run.

26. D. M. FERRY & COS. CELEBRATED SEEDS.
Lithographer: Calvert Lithographing & Engraving Co., Detroit, about 1880. 32 x 23.

The Detroit firm of D. M. Ferry, importers and growers of fine seeds, surrounded the rustic wood letters of "Seeds" with advertisements for its Premium Cabbage, Purple Top Strap Leaved Turnip and Improved Yellow Swede or Rutabaga. The company was established by Dexter M. Ferry in 1856 and was incorporated in 1879. While the firm's office, store and warehouses were in the city, its seed farm and garden were a quarter mile outside the city limits. D. M. Ferry vied with other seed companies in printing attractive and colorful posters that became popular wall decorations in the barns, sheds, kitchens and outhouses of rural America. In 1930 the firm merged with C. C. Morse of California, forming the Ferry-Morse Seed Co., with headquarters in Mt. View, California, and a Packet Division in Fulton, Kentucky.

On the Calvert Co., see the note to page 14.

27. D. M. FERRY & CO'S STANDARD SEEDS.
Lithographer: American Lithographic Co., New York, about 1890. 25⅝ x 13½.

In a borrowing from Mark Twain, this view of an early fence decorator in action puts forward the excellence of D. M. Ferry & Co.'s seeds. This straightforward message is unlike most posters for seeds, which emphasize the botanical marvels that may be grown from even standard seeds. The American Lithographic Co. was located at 37 City Hall Place.

28. COLUMBIA BICYCLES AND TRICYCLES.
Lithographers: Donaldson Brothers, New York, about 1885. 27⅞ x 12¾.

By 1885 the Pope Manufacturing Co. of Boston had extended its distribution of bicycles and adult tricycles to branch houses in New York and Chicago. Duplicates of this handsome poster, printed in New York and featuring the company's "Staunch and Reliable Roadsters," might be ordered by mail for 15¢ in stamps. In the foreground is seen an example of the Columbia tricycle, considered the most appropriate of the company's "popular steeds of today" for the woman rider.

In 1895 the Pope Manufacturing Co. relocated in Hartford; still interested in posters as an aid to sales, the firm advertised a contest in which the first prize was $100 and a Columbia bicycle, also worth $100. The prize-winning entry was by Maxfield Parrish of Philadelphia. The following year the work of 514 winners and runners-up were catalogued and exhibited by the company.

Almost the greatest influence of the Art Nouveau movement was the effect that it had on graphic design, and many of the entries in this contest demonstrate the dramatic change that greatly affected the appearance of advertising posters from 1895 onward. The asymmetrical flowing line of Art Nouveau and its derivations from Oriental design were admirably suited to lithographic reproduction, and the Columbia Bicycle contest reflected the new wave.

29. COLUMBIA BICYCLES.
Lithographer: Forbes Co., Boston, about 1886. 15⅝ x 11.

Seven bicycling feats are recorded in this poster illustrating the high-wheeled Columbia bicycle. The safety bicycle with low wheels of equal size was invented in 1889, and the beautiful, but old-fashioned, vehicles seen here were soon to be outmoded. The Pope Co. displays some appropriate accessories for the cyclist that could be purchased along with its "ever saddled horse which eats nothing."

The Forbes Lithography Manufacturing Co., at 181 Devonshire Street in Boston, specialized in photolithography and in steel-plate reproductions of popular and famous paintings. The Forbes Co. was among the first American firms to use this direct photomechanical process to make the albertype, named after its inventor, the German photographer Joseph Albert.

30. THE LAST DAYS OF POMPEII; MANHATTAN BEACH.
Artist: Jones. Lithographer: American Graphic Co., New York, 1885. 16⅝ x 25½.

With Pain's fireworks and Patrick Sarsfield Gilmore's gala concert band as part of the spectacular display to be seen at Manhattan Beach, the summer season there attracted crowds from the city for the very noisy and brilliant entertainment *The Last Days of Pompeii*. Gilmore called the summer of 1885 his jubilee, and his band of 65 men spent the celebration playing at this and other festivals at the popular New York beach resort. The preceding year, *The Storming of Pekin* aroused the "ohs" and "ahs" of the spectators; at the end of the 1885 season another attraction, *The Burning of Moscow*, was introduced to alternate with the wonders of *The Last Days of Pompeii*. These were examples of the theatrical spectacles so popular in the nineteenth century; in the twentieth they were superseded by their filmed counterparts.

Gilmore, also a composer (he probably wrote "When Johnny Comes Marching Home"), was the foremost bandmaster of his day; after his death both Sousa and Victor Herbert vied for the title.

31. ALVIN JOSLIN.
Artist: E. Roe (Emil Rothengatter). Lithographer: Strobridge Lithographing Co., Cincinnati, 1885. 19¼ x 26¾.

This hayseed comedy opened at the Windsor Theatre, New York, in June 1882, with the star of the company, Charles L. Davis, in the title role. How often it supplied the "180 laughs" in New York is a matter for conjecture, since its real popularity was in small communities. However, the show did appear at a number of New York houses: in 1882 it was presented in the first season of the Mount Morris Theatre on 131st Street; in 1883 it was at the People's Theatre (for the first week in June), then went on to the stages of the Windsor and the Lee Avenue Academy of Music in the Williamsburgh section of Brooklyn. For several years following its opening, the play was the only vehicle in which Davis appeared, leading the theatre historian Odell to typify this combination of actor and role as "inevitable."

The artist Emil Rothengatter designed the municipal flag of Cincinnati, the metropolis where the Strobridge Co. originated and had its principal base.

32 & 33. THE GREAT ATLANTIC & PACIFIC TEA CO.
New York, 1886. 20¼ x 29.

The Great Atlantic and Pacific Tea Co. first appears in New York directories at 191 Fulton Street in 1873, although the firm was established in 1861 by John H. Hartford as the Great American Tea Company with headquarters on Vesey Street. A. & P. originally sold its cargo lots of teas through groups or clubs, eliminating the middleman and retail outlet; the firm advertised that their products were from "the best tea districts of China and Japan." By 1886 the firm had added Sultana Coffee to its line and this beverage, along with the familiar tea, is prominently featured in the pandemonium illustrated here. While Washington and Lincoln serenely view the madhouse, throngs of customers—all male, all white—are served with great dispatch by exclusively black waiters. The scene is governed by a figure, far left, looking more like Edward VII than like a train conductor, typifying the era when watches might be set by train departures. In this case the steam is up and two minutes remain before the diamond-stack engine leaves the station.

34. HILL BROTHERS, MILLINERY GOODS.
Lithographers: Sackett, Wilhelms & Betzig, New York, about 1885. 25⅝ x 38.

The interior of the Hill Brothers' millinery and straw-goods store on Broadway provides a delightful poster subject. The forms of mountains of hat bodies, endless reels of ribbon, bolts of fabric and stacks of boxes establish a charming repeat pattern. Nineteenth-century order prevails in more than the stock; all the salesmen are men, most of the customers are women. The cashier's desk and offices are to the right, between stairs at the front of the store and an elevator at the end of the glass and panel-enclosed wall. Of special note is the large spread eagle that rises above the cashier's sign. In 1884 and 1885 four brothers ran the business: Stanley, Sylvester, William and Philip; all four Hills lived in Brooklyn.

The firm of Sackett & Wilhelms is still in operation in Carle Place, Long Island.

35. THE J. M. BRUNSWICK & BALKE CO.
Lithographers: Kurz & Allison, Chicago, about 1885. 22⅝ x 32¼.

Three fashionably dressed ladies and an agile girl demonstrate their prowess at billiards under the watchful eyes of five company officers in the group portrait hanging on the wall. (On their table is a cast-metal double inkwell with small antlers to hold two pens.)

John M. Brunswick, Cincinnati cabinetmaker, made the first billiard table in America in 1845. In 1882, he joined with Julius Balke to organize a company which today, as Brunswick, Balke, Collender Co., is one of the largest manufacturers of bowling and billiard equipment in the United States.

At about the time that the first partners were making this gorgeous table supported by a small pride of ebonized and gilded lions, they were "sole manufacturers and patentees of the Standard, Monarch, Non-Pareil, Novelty and the famous Eclipse Billiard and Pool Tables." In a room notable for rich overlays of Victorian design, the gas chandeliers and sideboard (constructed as a cue holder and tally rack) can hardly compete with the company's table. In 1886, both J. M. Brunswick and Julius Balke lived in Cincinnati's fashionable Walnut Hills and, less than ten years after its invention, had telephones in their homes. It is tempting to imagine these instruments in billiard rooms similar to the one in the poster.

36. HALSTEAD & CO., BEEF AND PORK PACKERS.
Lithographer: H. Bencke, New York, 1886. 20½ x 26⅝.

This extraordinary lower New York river view shows five Manhattan cowboys in a street roundup of cattle and hogs. The Halstead Co. had outlets in the Produce Exchange and a location on the east side of Forsyth Street between Stanton and Houston. The vignette of Mount Vernon, upper right, illustrates the trade name of the company's hams. The company shipped its long-keeping smoked and salted meats to both foreign and domestic markets.

NOTES TO THE PLATES 103

37. *THE REMINGTON FIRE ENGINE,
HOWE'S PATENTS.*
*Lithographer: Charles Gies & Co., Buffalo,
about 1890. 17¼ x 22½.*

The plant of the Remington Agricultural Co. was located on the opposite side of the Erie Canal from the Remington Armory in Ilion, New York (see note to page 75). Manufacture of plows, horseshoes, cultivators and the American Needle Cotton Gin and Condenser taught the Remington pattern makers and machinists many of the techniques that were incorporated into the mechanical octopus illustrated here, the Remington Hose Cart. Another of the firm's products was the Whipple Patent Iron Bridge, mentioned in a company history of 1872 as "generally adopted by the canals of the country, the Erie alone having over 600."

The pictured view does not conform to the townscape of Ilion, although it is tempting to identify the fire as the only major conflagration to take place there in the late nineteenth century, the burning of the Maben Opera House on First Street in April 1878.

The Howe's patents mentioned in the title are identified by the Remington Gun Museum as those of B. J. C. Howe.

38. *THE "HOFFMAN HOUSE" BOUQUET CIGAR.*
*Lithographer: Knapp Co., New York,
about 1893. 25¾ x 31¼.*

At about the time that this gathering of distinguished men took place in the opulent lobby of the Hoffman House, the hotel was described as follows:

> A peculiar feature of New York is its hotels which perhaps surpass in number, extent and the expensiveness of their equipment those of any city in the world. Among the most famous of these—an acknowledged leader—is the Hoffman House. It is located in the very heart of the fashionable quarter of the city, directly opposite the beautiful Madison Square, close to the art galleries and other resorts of the elite . . . by its patrons [it] is said to be the best Hotel in the world.

In the men's bar off the lobby Adolphe William Bouguereau's painting of naked nymphs was a titillating part of the decor.

The Foster-Hilson Co., makers of Bouquet Cigars, operated from locations at 667 First Avenue and 529 Broadway. Further down Broadway was the firm of Knapp Co.; Joseph P. Knapp, its president, also maintained a lithography shop at 56 Park Place. He was undoubtedly a son or nephew of Joseph F. Knapp, a lithographer in New York in the 1860s (see note to page 11).

The lithographer seems to have concocted this gathering of worthies from individual photographs of the subjects. Standing to the left of goateed Indian scout and showman Buffalo Bill Cody is the Honorable Thomas Witherell Palmer, merchant, senator, diplomat and president of the 1893 World's Columbian Exposition of Chicago. Right of Buffalo Bill, Grover Cleveland exchanges pleasantries with Chauncey M. Depew, lawyer, railroad president and U.S. senator. At center stage stands Tony Pastor, rotund actor and theatre manager, who holds a cane (and smokes a cigar that must surely be the Hoffman House brand). The handsome bearded man to his left is Max Hilson himself, secretary of the Foster-Hilson Co. In a derby hat, immediately in back of the elegant cigar lighter, is the house detective, while (far right) actor Nat Goodwin selects one of the fine cigars featured in this poster.

Other luminaries present are the politician David Bennett Hill, a U.S. senator at the time of this poster; General John McAllister Schofield, one of the three army commanders during the Atlanta campaign of Sherman, whom he succeeded in 1888 as commanding general of the U.S. Army; and the preeminent stage magician Alexander Herrmann.

39. *ESTEY ORGAN CO.*
About 1890. 17½ x 24.

Late in the nineteenth century, the Estey Organ Co. advertised "the most extensive organ works in the world" and a print or painting of its factory hangs in a position second only to Beethoven's portrait in a Victorian parlor graced by the presence of an Estey "Cottage Organ." In this period the firm had been in business in Brattleboro, Vermont, for almost 25 years.

By 1890, the Esteys had two New York locations: piano warehouses at 5 East 14th Street, just west of Union Square (then the center of musical-instrument dealers in the city), and a location one block from the East River on 62nd Street, where its building, probably another warehouse, was flanked by gasworks to the east and coal and stone yards to the south.

The small party gathering for a musical evening hear and see not only the superiority of the "tone, durability and finish" of the Estey organ, but are further entertained by selections from the *Estey Organ Method.*

40. *PRIMROSE & WEST'S BIG MINSTREL FESTIVAL.*
*Lithographer: Strobridge Lithographing Co.,
Cincinnati & New York, 1894. 11 x 16.*

Primrose & West's Minstrels, one of the major minstrel aggregations in the country, were unusual in casting a large number of blacks in their revues, as advertised here. Many companies used only a few black stars, if any, and utilized whites in blackface for most of their acts.

The specialty illustrated in the poster is most likely *Monte Carlo*, set for January 8 to 13, 1894, at Holmes' Star Theatre. The play was termed "enigmatic" by George Odell, historian of the New York stage; certainly the Elizabethan costumes and fourteen black and white interlocutors are enigma enough.

41. *HAWES & GRAHAM; MAHOGANY
& ROSE WOOD.*
*Artist & lithographer: Leopold Grozelier.
Printers: Louis Nagel & Adam Weingärtner,
New York, about 1850. 16¾ x 12⅜.*

This lovely monochromatic poster is a small encyclopedia of inner-city culture at mid-century. The bustle of life along the cobbled street, architecture and usage of commercial and residential buildings, business signage, office decorum, shop-entrance design, men's and women's fashions and transportation by horsecar are all recorded in detail. The openness of P. Weiler's Fancy Moulding Shop is worth remarking, as is the spillover of business onto the cut-stone sidewalk. Surely the top-hatted proprietor at the open door of 176 Centre Street must be either Mr. Hawes or Mr. Graham, whose stock "embraces the most extensive variety of finely Figured Woods to be found in the United States, viz:— Mahogany, Rose Wood – Satin – Zebra – Ebony – Oak – Spanish & Red Cedar – White Holly – Walnut – Maple & Spruce." The building at 174 Centre Street is a first-class brick building and appears to be a residence with a fine winding staircase to the upper floors. South toward Walker Street was an open mahogany yard, located at numbers 164, 166 and 168.

42. *FRESH OYSTERS!; AMBOY LINE.*
*Printer: Fairmans' Job Printing Office,
Elmira, 1853. 13¼ x 10⅜.*

This delightful small poster, with handsome type and a typographic border surrounding Devereux & Brown's sprightly woodcut, suggests the means for conveying oysters fresh from the New Jersey shore to points along the Susquehanna and Chenango River valleys west to Binghamton and north to Utica. The Fairman firm used one of Richard Hoe's cylinder power presses and also one of the same company's ruling machines.

The oysters jog along behind the engine and coal tender in their own little mobile icehouse, its height providing passengers in the open-ended wooden railway car some protection from the heavy smoke billowing from the stack. Somehow the cooled and protected mollusks seem to have the advantage over the fashionably dressed passengers, but perhaps progress was leisurely along these beautiful stretches of New York landscape, and the level track preferable to horse carriages traversing a dirt road.

43. MOFFAT'S VEGETABLE LIFE PILLS AND PHOENIX BITTERS.
Probably New York, about 1860. 23⅞ x 17¼.

This poster, with a repeat border of double cornucopias, demonstrates the attractiveness of mid nineteenth-century type. A variety of simple faces are used, organized into a pleasing and harmonious design that is a contrast to the complaints that the blood-purifying effects of Life Pills and Phoenix Bitters might cure. In developing his vegetable medicines, Dr. Moffat directed his attention to "Planters, Farmers, and Others" and to the fevers and agues that were the "scourge of the western country." Moffat advised his customers that his preparations were more effective against mercurial diseases "than the most powerful preparation of Sarsaparilla" and equally helpful in the cure of scrofula or King's Evil "in its worst forms."

44. DR. JOHN WESLEY KELLEY'S DIAMOND PECTORAL.
Probably New York, 1852. 16⅝ x 11⅝.

Even though the type is raggedly printed, interesting design and careful organization are exhibited in the foliate shield and central illustration in the poster for Dr. John Wesley Kelley's nostrum for diseases of the throat and chest. The pleasant Victorian room in which "Mother is Saved!" is typical of many New York interiors of the period. The drama of the scene arises from the unanswered questions it presents: was it Holy Writ or Diamond Pectoral that brought the invalid back to life? And who are the figures from the outside world (center) bearing a message of salvation to the praying youth?

45. THOMPSON'S FOLDING LIFE PRESERVING SEAT.
Artist: T. B. (probably Thomas Benecke). Lithographers: Louis Nagel & Adam Weingärtner, New York, 1854. 21⅝ x 17.

One of the most imaginatively conceived posters in the Landauer Collection is this advertisement for Thompson's Folding Life Preserving Seat. The seat's design is illustrated in rope-bordered vignettes. It is revealed in triumphant and successful use in the central picture, where the wooden folding device is shown to be as neatly contrived as the poster that advertises it. The eagle-borne ribbon at the top left names the inventor as Nathan Thompson. In 1858 and 1859 New York directories a Nathan Thompson appears as a purveyor of life preservers, with a shop located close by the docks that lined the East River at South Street. He is designated as the second of his name, and it is probable that he is the son of the Nathan Thompson listed in the 1840 directory as a "carpenter." The father was very likely the inventor of the seat advertised here.

Thomas Benecke is identified as the artist by his use of a similar monogram device in fully signing his last name to a fine poster featuring Barnum's Museum that was issued by the same lithographers the following year.

46 left: GRIFFIN AND CHRISTY'S MINSTRELS.
Printer: Herald Job Print, New York, 1867. 21⅛ x 7¼.

Right: BARNUM'S AMERICAN MUSEUM.
Printer: Herald Job Print, New York, 1856. 21 x 7¼.

Famous names in mid nineteenth-century entertainment presented the two variety bills illustrated. Both were run by Herald Job Print with Barnum and Tom Thumb's poster preceding Griffin and Christy's Minstrels by more than ten years. The two performances bracket the Civil War and demonstrate a general Yankee interest in the black experience. Although the Barnum ad devotes half its front side to wonders of the American Museum's menagerie and sideshow, the reverse is given exclusively to Tom Thumb's appearance in blackface as Tom Tit in the great moral drama of *Dred*, a play based on Harriet Beecher Stowe's 1856 novel *Dred: A Tale of the Great Dismal Swamp*. Tom Tit is "a singular and unique juvenile specimen . . . continually going to glory." The little general also acted as director of "the troubadours of Magnolia Grove."

Early minstrel shows and mid-century melodramas with music forecast entertainments like Griffin and Christy's with its four-part program. Conversation and music by the minstrel troupe was followed by specialty acts and orchestral selections and concluded with the farcical "Statue Lover." The unusual feature of the program advertised here was the appearance of Japanese jugglers, possibly another ethnic assumption on the part of the minstrel troupe. Genuine Japanese jugglers had been brought to America just the year before, by special arrangement with the Mikado's government, and had created a sensation in the variety theatre.

47. MAY CARLETON'S LAST TRIUMPH! GIPSY GOWER OR THE STAR OF THE VALLEY!
Artist: Richard Shugg. Publisher: New York Mercury, New York, 1859. 43¾ x 27¾.

This romantic tale by "Cousin" May Carleton transports the reader from New York to the middle states in the "wild and unfathomable mystery that surrounds . . . the heroine." The prolific illustrator Felix O. C. Darley illustrated the "Tales and Romances" that appeared serially in the *New York Mercury* of 1859, but the Brooklyn engraver Richard Shugg provided the dramatic woodcut illustrating this poster for the commencement of a winter's tale in "the largest, handsomest, and most beautifully illustrated story paper in the world." The published assertion that U.S. postmasters could buy and resell the *Mercury* suggests that conflict of interest among civil servants was not an issue of particular concern on the eve of the Civil War.

48. B. RATHBUN CARRIAGE MANUFACTURER, BUFFALO.
Lithographer: George Endicott, New York, about 1860. 22½ x 17⅞.

Nineteen carriages grace this beautiful poster lithographed by George Endicott of New York for Benjamin Rathbun of

NOTES TO THE PLATES 105

Buffalo. Rathbun is listed as as a ship joiner in late 1840s directories and as a "builder" in the 1860s, the apparent period of this fine black-and-white design.

From the elegant lines of the mail coach at the top through barouche, caleche, phaeton and chaise, Rathbun identifies a wide range of carriage designs as his shop's output. Almost as interesting as the fine carriages are the elegant "horses" supporting the traces.

49. WESTCHESTER STOVE WORKS.
Probably New York, 1858. 21¾ x 17.

The marvelous creations of the Westchester Stove Works were manufactured at New, Ewell & Co.'s foundry in Westchester County, but were sold in Manhattan from the smallish first-class brick building at 69 Warren Street that was the company's New York store.

The "new" patterns illustrated were "selected with a view to utility, simplicity in operation, and perfectness in construction and durability." The names of the parlor, kitchen and laundry stoves are as delightful as the designs. For the kitchen, the Home Companion "will be found to be the most Condensed and satisfactory Cooking Apparatus yet introduced," although its oven was probably not comparable to the large one in Crown of the West, a wood stove with long firebox. While the Radiator probably worked well as a coal stove in the parlor, the elaborately designed Elizabethan Parlor was equipped to burn either wood or coal. Connecticut was a large square all-business model for the kitchen; Cottage Home, a smaller, fancier version of the same stove, was designed to burn only wood. The Peace Maker, covered with patriotic designs, would have ornamented a laundry or kitchen in any one of its five sizes.

50. BEAUTIFULLY ILLUMINATED SHOWCARDS FOR EVERY BUSINESS.
Lithographers: James A. Shearman & Charles H. Hart, New York, about 1863. 17¼ x 21⅝.

While lithographers Hart and Shearman worked within a few doors of each other on Fulton Street (see note to page 10), only Hart is listed in city directories at the 99 Fulton Street address. Both men lived in Brooklyn, Shearman on Washington Avenue and Hart on Schermerhorn Street. Some of the show cards, portraits, landscapes, buildings, views of hotels, music titles, labels, maps, plans, "fac simile circulars," bill heads, "&c. &c." that they advertised as their specialty in New York's *Commercial Register* appear in miniature surrounding the rustic type in which their firm name is set. Laurel-framed Washington, most favored of all American subjects, is the central vignette, but displays of nineteenth-century wearing apparel, machinery and transportation, set forth like fancy labels on a lacy Valentine, provide an index to the partners' talents.

51. COLT'S PATENT FIRE ARMS MANUFACTORY.
Lithographer: L. Schierholz, Hartford, about 1862. 16 x 21⅛.

The giant gilded colt weathervane atop the onion dome of the factory on Vandyke Avenue on the east bank of the Connecticut River is a familiar Hartford landmark today. The lithographer who did this view of the preceding Colt factory (at the same location) provides graphic evidence of the beauty and utility of mid nineteenth-century American manufacturing plants and their outbuildings, and the similarity of the latter to the dependencies of great Southern plantations. Workers' tenements and the Colt Willow Ware Works are shown in the background at the left. The willow works were established to make wicker furniture from the abundant osier hedge that Samuel Colt planted along the river to hold and strengthen the two-mile-long dike he constructed there.

The charming Victorian structure to the right, with veranda and gilded turret, is Charter Oak Hall, where Colt's Guard Armory and Colt's Armory Band were housed in 1860. It vanished, along with the diamond-paned windows in the covered walkway that connected hall and factory, when the armory burned in 1864. The present building, similar in design to the original plant (although embellished with a blue rather than a starred and gilded dome), dates from 1867. Today ribbons of superhighway loop, knot, loosen and entwine where this rutted country road at South Meadows once accommodated pedestrians, carts and carriages in leisurely fashion.

52. RALPH & CO.; UNION AGRICULTURAL WORKS.
Artist: Elisha Forbes. Lithographer: Richard H. Pease, Albany, about 1855. 25 x 19.

While the poster illustrates two facades of Ralph & Co.'s Union Agricultural Works, near the East River at 23 Fulton Street in New York, and the farming implements offered for sale there, the design, lithography and chief invention are all Albany products. The explanation is to be found in Emery & Co.'s "Improved Rail Road Horse Power & Over Shot Thresher." The exhibition of this Albany-produced horse treadmill outside Mechanic's Hall at the State Agricultural Fair is the lead illustration; its use in the field is shown in the lower illustration, within a border enlivened with agricultural symbols and pastoral vignettes. The medals won at the fair by the treadmill hang above the bottom view.

Elisha Forbes, the artist, is listed as a "draughtsman" in Albany directories. Shortly after executing this poster he moved to Manhattan, where, in 1860, he was listed as a designer. The lithographer was Richard Pease, whose shop was in the Temple of Fancy, a store on Broadway in Albany.

Horace Emery established Emery & Co., later known as the Albany Agricultural Works, in the late 1840s. He was superintendent and manager under both firm names, and it seems likely that he developed the horse-powered machine celebrated here.

53. GEORGE HART, PLAIN & ORNAMENTAL SLATE ROOFER.
Lithographers: James A. Shearman & Charles H. Hart, New York, about 1864. 20⅝ x 16½.

This elegant poster with architectural ornament and detail is an example of the fine lithography done by the firm of Shearman & Hart. While 1864 is the earliest listing for George Hart, roofer, at the 54 Roosevelt Street address, it is also the first time in several years in which the name of James A. Shearman does not appear in New York city directories, although his partner is still listed.

Whether Charles Hart, "practical lithographer," and George Hart, "plain & ornamental slate roofer," were related is unknown, but the poster is a well-organized example of the genre. The house is typical of the cottages and villas designed by Alexander Jackson Davis; the original ornamental slate-roof design, combining Hart's octagon and plain slates, shows how effectively the lacework of a Victorian facade might be repeated in the roof of the structure. The metal cornices and "Washington" and "American Cottage" slate designs testify to the engaging variety of pattern available to architects and builders in this period.

*54. NEW-YORK HISTORICAL SOCIETY.
LECTURES ON EGYPT.
New York, 1864. 43¼ x 25.*

Late in 1860 the Society acquired the approximately 1100 Egyptian objects amassed by Dr. Henry Abbott, a British physician who had become enamored of Egyptian culture during a twenty-year residence in that country. Dr. Abbott died in 1859, and final payment for what was then the greatest Egyptian collection in America was made to his estate. By April 1861, the collection of sculpture, jewels and other art and archeological objects was on view in the Society's building at the corner of East 11th Street and Second Avenue.

The lecture advertised here took place at Cooper Institute, close by; on at least one occasion during this 1864 series, lecturers and attendants walked from the Institute to the Society for punch and oysters following the talk. The occasion of the "Unrolling of the Mummy" may have made such a collation inadvisable.

In 1917 the society's Egyptian collection, including two colossal mummified bulls, was placed on view in Dexter Hall in the Society's present building. As new wings were added in the 1930s the collection was placed on permanent loan and was later purchased by the Brooklyn Museum. Today many of these Egyptian objects may be seen in that museum's collections.

*55 left: JOHN O'BRIEN'S SIX SHOWS
CONSOLIDATED.
Artist, wood engraver & printer: James
Reilley, New York, 1866. 24¾ x 8⅝.*

*Right: THE ORIGINAL AND WORLD FAMED
WILD WEST AND GREAT FOREPAUGH SHOWS.
Printer: Morrell Show Print, Philadelphia,
1888. 27¼ x 9⅝.*

In the poster for John O'Brien's Six Shows Consolidated, a glorious circus parade weaves its way from distant horse-drawn wagons at the top of the page down to the show's elephants and an arcaded bandwagon drawn by an incredible team of forty horses. The performance advertised took place in Chelsea (the New York City neighborhood or the town in Vermont), and, if the reality even approached the circus bill, O'Brien's "Gorgeous Parade in all its Glory" must have made that Tuesday, July 19, a splendid occasion for the spectators who lined the way.

Even as the circus attracted urban dwellers, the combined Wild West and Great Forepaugh Shows drew out-of-towners into the city, and railroad schedules and arrangements for traveling to the combined shows are listed on the back of the bill. Adam Forepaugh's "Picaninny, The Famous Clown Elephant," is seen just below the spectacle of Custer's Battle of Little Big Horn. The ropewalking horse Blondin (its name derived from the intrepid French ropewalker who first crossed Niagara Falls in 1859) is also portrayed. Women sharpshooters, riders and ropers are featured in the woodcut at the bottom, supplied to Morrell Show Print by the Courier Co. in Buffalo.

*56. SUPPLEMENT TO FASHIONS FOR 1867–68,
BY H. CLAYS.
New York, 1867. 17¼ x 22¼.*

Advertisements for suppliers to H. Clays's men's fashions store appear almost as painted wings on a scene borrowed from nineteenth-century melodrama. The youth with his back to the audience, and bow and arrow in hand, appears as a youthful villain, even though he wears a splendid overcoat trimmed with soutache braid. The slim, mustachioed young man, far right, covertly inspecting the wide-eyed innocence of the central quartet, does nothing to dispel the sense of drama. However, the ribbons of type that garland the scene speak with so much good sense and business logic of cassimeres and vestings, fine woolens, sewing silk, machine twist and a revolving button riveter that perhaps this is after all just one way to establish the magnificence of Victorian men's dress in the late 1860s. An early blow for the liberation of women may be seen, lower left, in the flat declaration, "One Girl's work equal to 12 Men!!"

*57. ELECTRIC EXTRACTOR.
Lithographer: Charles H. Hart, New York,
about 1870. 16 x 21⅛.*

The posters issued by Hart's lithography plant, located at the northeast corner of Fulton and William Streets, are among the most imaginative and best designed in a period of great advertising posters that began about 1840 and lasted with little change to about 1895. Here borders, background, type and illustrations are integrated into a pleasing design with a selling message. Today, labeled bottles with glass stoppers like those seen here are antiques prized by bottle collectors; but even as the poster was created, the bottles of "Electric Extractor" were presented as works of art and displayed in shell-carved niches. Despite the trade title which, sans illustration, might conjure up a picture of a whirling machine to extract moisture from wet wash, this 1869 invention of C. B. Skiff was for the removal of "Paint, Oil, Tar, Varnish, Grease, Ink and Fruit Stains from Garments and all Silk, Woolen and Linen fabrics." At the center, the product is demonstrated on men's and women's clothes and on a drop-in customer with a spot on his shoulder.

Despite the patent registration in New Jersey, the firm was located in New York in 1870; both the president and cashier of the company—M. F. Braisted and C. O. Manny—had houses in Yonkers.

*58. CROSBY, BUTTERFIELD & HAVEN,
MANUFACTURERS OF ROPER'S CALORIC ENGINE.
Lithographer: Rae Smith, New York,
about 1868. 22¼ x 16½.*

The pride that the nineteenth-century manufacturer took in new and complex machines that increased efficiency and production is exemplified in this poster advertising the merits of Roper's caloric engine. The output of the sculptural marvel is apparently set to use in the belt-operated nailing and pegging machines, left and right. Other steps in boot and shoe manufacturing indicated in the remaining border illustrations include crimping, feather edging, wax threading and heel trimming.

The five-story factory of Crosby, Butterfield & Haven was located on Dey Street, one block south of St. Paul's Chapel between Church Street and Broadway. Although Rae Smith, the lithographer, operated a shop on Nassau Street, his home was in New Jersey.

*59. SPRING STYLES; TERRY HATS & FURS.
Lithographers: Richard Major & Joseph F.
Knapp, New York, 1867. 21¾ x 17½.*

This springtime advertisement for John R. Terry's hat and fur store, on the west side of Broadway south of Canal Street, combines a number of diverse elements in pleasing and harmonious fashion. The poster was produced by Major &

Knapp (see notes to pages 11 and 12), the large printing firm specializing in advertising posters, located in this period just south of Trinity Church.

The vignettes, bound together by a beautiful border of stylized leaves, indicate appropriate headgear for equestrian outings or promenades. Four trimmed ladies' hats are enfolded into the border, while children's hats and a topper punctuate the title that arches over a cut of the Terry storefront. The intricacies of 1867 fashion are illustrated in trimmed chapeaux that cover a wide range of fashion from "Star" for infants (its rosettes and wide ribbons suggesting an Oriental inspiration) to the interlaced streamers of "Henrietta" (No. 12) designed to top and complete a costume with a bustled skirt. By 1870, John Terry relocated his store, moving to Union Square, an indication that New York's fashion center was moving uptown as the city developed.

60. INDIAN COMPOUND.
Lithographer: Charles H. Hart, New York, about 1870. 21¼ x 15⅜.

Indian remedies were popular nineteenth-century folk medicines that ranged fron the Indian Weed—today called marijuana—to this nostrum for cough, colds and other "affections" of the throat and lungs. Two herbs were combined with honey into a soothing syrup advertised for New York respiratory ailments. The bare-chested Indian gathering herbs at her teepee door sets a fantasy in motion of individual bottle-by-bottle preparation of fresh-squeezed boneset flowers, honey and dried scales of the squill bulb. Squill, in the lily family, was used as an expectorant, heart stimulant and diuretic. Selection of the proper "Squills" would have been imperative, for the red-bulbed strain was used as a poison to kill rats.

The large type employed by the Hart lithographers is varied and beautiful, the largest blocks repeating the line of Indian tents beneath a sunny "Indian Compound" arch of sky.

61. THE CELEBRATED WILD CHERRY TONIC.
Windsor, Vermont, about 1876. 25 x 18⅜.

This lively all-type poster is outstanding for boldness of letters and for pleasing organization of several sizes and varieties of type. Words printed in red and black convey the restorative powers of the tonic they celebrate. The Vermont apothecary Milton K. Paine was active in another pursuit involving printing; he was one of the founders of the town's library, and president of the Windsor Library Association. The library, which opened to the public on June 23, 1883, was housed in the basement of Windsor's town hall.

62 left: GILMORE'S GARDEN.
Printer: W. H. Giffing, New York, 1892. 40 x 12¾.

Right: WOOD'S MUSEUM; BUFFALO BILL.
Printer: Merrihew & Son, Philadelphia, 1872. 41¾ x 13⅜.

Long flamboyant broadsides advertise two Wild West entertainments in New York. Cowboys, Indians and Mexicans star in feats of horsemanship, combined with energetic recreations of Indian life and trotting, running and ladies' flat races in a late nineteenth-century on-stage rodeo at Gilmore's Garden. The New York theatre here called Gilmore's was, in fact, Niblo's Garden at Broadway and Prince Street; the following season it reverted to its original name as Gilmore's lease expired and Alexander C. Comstock took over the house from the heirs of A. T. Stewart. The Garden survived until 1895, but finally fell before the northward movement of the city's population.

Twenty years earlier, and not so active as the cowboy-and-Indian thriller at Gilmore's, was the presentation *Buffalo Bill*, from Ned Buntline's weekly story, with J. M. Ward playing the "King of the Border Men." On Friday, November 15, 1872, the starring actor was awarded a benefit performance. Fourteen years later Ward returned to this role in a performance noted as his first appearance in eleven years. Buffalo Bill played himself in another dramatization of his career.

63. VROLYKE KERSTYD! GELUKKIG NIEUWJAAR!
Wood engraver: W. Howland, New York, 1873 & 1877. 21 x 13⅜.

The title is Dutch for "Merry Christmas! Happy New Year!" Four years after C. F. A. Hinrichs copyrighted the wood engraving seen on this poster, he used it to extend holiday good wishes to customers of his wholesale and retail toy, glass and fancy-goods store on the northwest corner of Park Place at Church Street. The Christmas figure is particularly interesting, more in the spirit of the New World Dutch and German Pelsnickle, or Nicholas-in-furs, than the jolly red-clad Santa Claus created by Thomas Nast who appeared some years later in the pages of *Harper's Weekly*. Unlike Pelsnickle, however, who beat bad children or left twigs in their shoes, this Santa carries only toys in his pack and fills stockings in the spirit of Clement Moore's "right jolly old elf." However, the gleam in his eye and his head-first loading of doll into stocking may be traces left over from the folk figure transferred to America who met mischief with further mischief.

Although the New York toy merchant C. F. A. Hinrichs noted that his business was established in 1801, he is not listed in New York directories until 1837.

64. I FEED YOU ALL!
Lithographer: American Oleographic Co., Milwaukee, 1875. 16½ x 22.

This delightful poster, celebrating the role of the nation's farmer and his relation to a number of other professions, was one of a number of similar designs prepared for the nation's centennial; another was made for use by members of the Grange.

Surrounding the prosperous, nattily clad farmer in his expensive boots are several vignettes; the leading ones, at the top on both sides of the arch, are assigned to Ulysses S. Grant as president and victorious Civil War general. Doctor, lawyer, stockbroker, moneylender, railroad tycoon, storekeeper, minister and shipowner turn to the farmer, who proclaims, "I Feed You All!"

The design and organization of the poster are beautiful, with rustic leafy trellis and draped bannerets reminiscent of a medieval book of hours. The illustrations are in the same spirit—a neo-Gothic fancy for the nation's hundredth birthday.

65. STEPHEN D. BARNES & CO., OYSTER PLANTERS & WHOLESALE DEALERS.
New York, about 1868. 14⅞ x 21⅜.

The view is of the oyster barges more or less permanently anchored along the East River on New York's East Street between Broome and DeLancey Streets at Oliver Slip. Most of the two-story barges are guarded by benevolent, top-hatted, frock-coated overseers. The wagons loaded with baskets of oysters and the snap and polish of almost bare warehouses speak of a flourishing business in oysters from New York and

108 NOTES TO THE PLATES

New Jersey waters. The forest of masts behind the barges further reflects the tonging and transporting of the succulent mollusks from oyster grounds to market.

Many of the oyster dealers maintained family businesses at this location for years, with sons frequently joining their fathers' companies. The main advertiser, Stephen Barnes, had another outlet in Fulton Market, but lived on Staten Island.

Worthy of special notice is the watchman's tiny one-story building on the pier at the right. William Churchill is listed in the 1868 New York directory as having his watchman's office on the East River at Pier 57 and a house in Brooklyn.

66. TRY RICE'S SEEDS.
Lithographer: Cosack & Co., Buffalo & Chicago, about 1870. 26⅛ x 18⅞.

Caricature and exaggeration, two elements of comic illustration, mark this exuberant poster for "The Best Cabbage in the World."

The producer of True Early Winningstadt was Jerome Bonaparte Rice, son of Roswell Niles Rice, who began a seed business in Salem, New York, in 1834. In 1844 the father located in Cambridge, New York, joining the established garden and vegetable-seed business of his uncle, Roswell Rice, and Simeon Crosby and his sons.

Jerome B. Rice joined the firm in 1865 after serving in the Civil War. In that conflict he rose from private to second lieutenant, and saw battle at Chancellorsville, Gettysburg and Atlanta, and participated in Sherman's march to the sea.

In his first years at the Cambridge Valley Seed Gardens the young man was its only salesman, traveling by horse and carriage from town to town in northern New York. In a 1901 history of Washington County, Jerome B. Rice is pictured; the resemblance between that middle-aged man and the jolly seedman, grappling with a giant cabbage in this poster, is marked. The wooden shoes and calabash pipe shown here speak of French and Dutch influence in Washington County, and the foraging cap recalls Rice's Civil War experience.

67. KANADESAGA NURSERIES OF
E. B. RICHARDSON & CO.
Artists: W. Scranton, New York; A. Blanc, Philadelphia; J. Miller. About 1875. 25¾ x 19.

A variety of woodcuts and lithographs of fruit and ornamental trees, berries, grapes, apples and roses decorate the border of this straightforward poster that includes an advertisement for agents to handle the fruit and ornamental stock of the Geneva nurseryman E. B. Richardson. The most beautiful of the cuts, the red raspberry pictured at the upper left, is by W. Scranton of New York, so far unlocated in New York directories of this period.

68. EDWD. RIDLEY & SONS, MILLINERY
& FANCY GOODS.
Lithographer: George Schlegel, New York, about 1875. 26½ x 20⅞.

Untrimmed straw-hat bodies for men, women and children skim like butterflies around the four stern black forms for men's felt hats in the staccato pattern surrounding the view of the Ridley straw-hat empire, at the southeast corner of Grand and Allen Streets. The firm occupied both the mansard-roofed and turreted frame structure in the center of the vignette and the two flat-roofed four- and five-story structures on Allen Street to the right of it.

Trimmings for the bonnet forms are suggested (upper right and left) and the New York woman of the mid-70s must have been hard pressed to choose among Duchess, Florette, Orleans, Camille and Rose Michel. The plain shapes conjure up romantic visions, too, in names like Opera, Audley, Jasmine, Columbia and Martha Washington, "the above shapes . . . made in French and Swiss chips, Milan, pedal, pearl, Coburg, Canton white black and imitation hair, in all colors and combinations, &c." The many floors containing the Ridleys' delightful fancy goods were "Accessible by Elevators"—both located in the buildings at the far right in the vignette.

69. "THE OLD" AND "THE NEW."
Wood engraver: W. Adrian, Pittsburgh, 1873. 22½ x 16⅞.

Illustrated are three nineteenth-century approaches to the Monday wash in a comic-Valentine black-and-white poster advertising J. C. Tilton's invention. The Steam Washer or Woman's Friend, at ten dollars, promised a farewell to wash-day blues. The features of the Women's Friend are exhibited (top left) in the kitchen of Sally and Bill White, identified in the verses that celebrate the invention (below). To the right, suffering through Monday with an old-style laundry boiler, are John and Jane Jacobin and their charming children, the girl named Minnie.

That the problem of another century's wash was a real one is demonstrated by some of the directions for the use of the improved washer (on the reverse of the poster): "Soak the clothes over night in warm suds—in the usual manner. Rinse, and put them through the wringer." In the morning a quarter bar of good soap is shaved into the bottom of the washer, a false bottom is placed over the soap, and water is added almost to the top of this plate: "Lay the clothes down smoothly, with the soiled parts well soaped . . . and carefully pack the clothes down," being sure that the kitchen stove is hot enough to generate steam in the washer. "When the water boils it will begin to flow up the tubes on the outside . . . after a steady circulation has been going on . . . for about thirty to forty minutes, the washing will be completed." To end Sally White's carefree day the clothes need only rinsing, wringing and hanging out to dry.

The washer was sold to agents at half the retail cost; numerous testimonials to its effectiveness, along with a rundown of the 1870 census, are also on the reverse side of the advertisement.

70. E. E. CONKLIN & CO., MANUFACTURERS
OF ICE TOOLS AND WAGONS.
Artist: John William Hill. Lithographer: possibly Smith Bros., New York, about 1875. 17⅝ x 22¼.

This beautifully organized poster was drawn by the landscape and topographical artist John William Hill, son of aquatint engraver John Hill. The artist made his home, from 1836 to his death in 1879, in West Nyack, New York, southwest of Rockland Lake, where E. E. Conklin's ice-manufacturing plant was located and where ice was cut and stored for the New York market. Interior and exterior views of the Conklin plant for manufacturing ice tools and wagons are surrounded by specialized tools for cutting and transporting ice. Similar tools may be seen in use in a small genre scene, by Andrew Fisher Bunner, of the Knickerbocker Ice Company's plant at Rockland Lake, in the New-York Historical Society's collection. Blocks of ice were stored in insulated warehouses on the shores of the lake and transported to the city in wagons manufactured by the Conklin Company (center right).

By 1874 Edward Conklin had a city establishment at 432

NOTES TO THE PLATES 109

Canal Street, in a building that ran through the block to Vestry Street. There he is listed as a dealer in ice, an indication that he was himself using the elegant tools and machinery pictured here.

71. METROPOLITAN CONCERT HALL.
Lithographer: Hopcraft & Co., New York, about 1880. 19¾ x 24⅝.

Many of the pleasures of a soft New York summer night are suggested in this poster showing an assembly gathering for a promenade concert at the then brand-new Metropolitan Concert Hall on Broadway at 41st Street and Seventh Avenue. The location was uptown from the part of the city where most entertainments were then presented, but Rudolph Aronson and his fifty musicians were an attraction that could draw an evening crowd. Landaus and hansoms bring theatregoers to the scene; top hats glisten in the waning light. The women's attire—tippets, and hooded and fringed fitted jackets—suggest that the time was near the end of the hall's first summer season, which began on May 27, 1880, Aronson's hundredth performance taking place at the new hall on September 21.

On either side of the frieze of faces that decorate the building may be seen the promenade. A café and restaurant were located on the premises, added inducements to an audience already attracted by the popular music offered by the Aronson orchestra.

In 1882, Aronson (also a composer) opened the Casino Theatre, a home of operetta and musical comedy until 1930.

72. BENJN. PAYN TOBACCONIST.
Artist: Charles Juehne. Lithographers: Weed, Parsons & Co., Albany, about 1875. 23 x 17.

About forty years after he had set himself up in the tobacco and chocolate business (see the early Payn & McNaughton poster on page 4), Benjamin Payn of Albany celebrated his success with a poster featuring the handsome building, at the corner of Maiden Lane and James Street, that he had enlarged in 1872. A variety of pipes and tobacco and chocolate products ornament the border of the poster, printed two blocks away at the plant of Weed, Parsons & Co. on Columbia Street, between Broadway and James Street. (In 1875 the partners in that enterprise were Thurlow Weed, J. D. Parsons, George Dawson and P. Ten Eyck.)

Painted shades and a colorful painted sign mark the shop window and two entrances to the building, its four upper floors devoted to manufacture and warehousing of the firm's products. Of special interest is the small-scale cigar-store figure set on the overhang between the first and second floors. Most American shop figures are larger than this, but Albany had already established a precedent in one of the earliest American cigar-store Indians known. Less than three feet high, probably carved by Ezra Ames, this figure, now owned by the Albany Institute of History and Art, was made for Caldwell & Solomons of Albany "at the sign of the Indian Chief and Hand of Tobacco." Payn's Indian appears to be a later creation, but the gilded hand holding tobacco leaves, directly above the street signs affixed to the building, agrees with the description in 1817 Albany advertisements for Caldwell & Solomons.

73. TYLER PATENT BATTING.
Lithographers: Donaldson Brothers, New York, about 1885. 22⅝ x 14.

Another scene from the entertaining, complex little domestic dramas presented in this collection of posters is illustrated in this advertisement for Tyler Patent Batting. Charles C. Tyler was the owner of the Tyler Batting and Warp Manufacturing Co. at 74 Franklin Street, New York.

The Victorian interior, decorated with more knicknacks than furniture, provides an admirable setting for the quilting party. The window is surrounded by a patterned, colored glass border, leaded at the corners. Calla lilies are in bloom in a Victorian vase on a whatnot stand next to a picture that suggests a genre scene by William A. Walker. The painting of a cotton field indicates the source for a major component of the yard-wide batting. The product's woven-gauze center provided strong support for a pieced quilt: this feature is demonstrated both by the energetic ladies framing the coverlet and the mischievous children and dog at play. Victorian carpeting and current styles are displayed to advantage, but only a glimpse of the top of the quilt is offered.

74. CABLE SCREW WIRE BOOTS & SHOES.
Artist: [probably James A.] Shearman. Lithographer: Peter Calvi, New York, about 1875. 19¼ x 15.

This poster shows the virtues of wearing Cable Screw Wire boots and shoes through the seasons of winter and spring. The elaborate initial letter forms part of the design separating vignettes of the two seasons. The company's medallic awards for its shoes, including one from Vienna in 1873, hang by ribbons from the holly-entwined C. The inconvenience of wearing lesser boots than the superior Cable Screw Wire variety is dramatized in the sledding scene at the top and in the ball-toss game below; in the latter view, help arrives in the person of an enterprising shoe salesman in his covered cart offering replacements for the damaged boot.

In the 1880 New York directory three members of the Cable family are listed as shoemakers; the only shop address is for Hiram W. Cable at 132 Duane, while shoemakers George D. and Samuel H. Cable have only their residences listed.

75. THE REMINGTON ARMORY, AND SEWING MACHINE WORKS.
About 1875. 31½ x 21.

Although sewing machines were exhibited at the Crystal Palace in London in 1851, it was not until the Paris Exhibition of 1867 that an improvement over his original invention brought a gold medal to Elias Howe. Development of the sewing machine progressed rapidly and a number of companies retooled their machine shops to produce these tailoring and sewing marvels; one of these was the Remington Armory, established in Ilion, New York, by Eliphalet Remington in 1828. Ilion was chosen as the site of the plant, seen at the bottom of the poster, because construction of the Erie Canal in the Mohawk Valley brought transportation within easy reach of the low one-story building that was the original Remington structure at this location. On the heights above the plant may be seen the Victorian mansion of Philo Remington.

In 1870, in a period of general peace, the Remington gun manufacturers turned their skills to development of a sewing machine. The first Remington machines demanded almost machinist skills to keep them in good running order. Soon designs were simplified, placing the operation within the capabilities of people like the Victorian mother and housewife pictured here, amiably stitching out the word "Remington" on her treadle machine. The view outside her window appears to be upriver, from the east bank of the Hudson near Fishkill.

110 NOTES TO THE PLATES

Another Remington product is illustrated on page 37: the hose cart manufactured by the Remington Agricultural Co., also in Ilion.

*76. G. W. PEABODY'S KINGSTON
ONE PRICE CLOTHING HOUSE.*
Printer: Nugent & Steves, New York,
about 1880. 51½ x 11⅞.

A carefully planned relation between woodcut and blocks of type appears in this handsome black-and-white poster. As in most nineteenth-century folk portraits of children, the boys are made to appear as miniature adults, wise beyond their years. Both men are nattily dressed in Peabody's Fine Ready-Made Clothing, but the dapper fellow to the right seems to have indulged in some of the gargantuan meals described in menus of that day. In 1880, the printers Nugent & Steves were listed for the last time in the New York City directories at the 195 Fulton Street address shown on the poster, moving to a new location on Pearl Street the following year. Their principal business was in sales of paper, but this poster shows that they either did printing themselves or commissioned work from a nearby printer's shop.

*77. POLYGAMY OR, THE MYSTERIES
OF MORMONISM.*
Printer: National Publishing Co., Philadelphia,
Chicago, St. Louis, Atlanta, 1882. 26 x 18.

Illustrated with some of the "nearly 100 fine engravings of life among the Mormons," this poster advertises the 572-page book that presented the Mormons in a sensational and highly unflattering light. Although the poster credits the Honorable O. J. Hollister, U.S. Revenue Collector for Utah, with authorship, the book's title page lists him as an assistant to J. H. Beadle, late editor of the *Salt Lake Reporter*, Utah correspondent of the *Cincinnati Commercial* and clerk of the Supreme Court for Utah. Beadle wrote of his own association with the Mormons to 1875 and then turned the remainder of the tale over to Hollister. In the book's preface, Beadle tells of visiting many of the locations associated with "Mormon Occupation" to collect material for his exposé.

The wood engravings are by different artists, working in a variety of styles; many of the most interesting are by J. Dalziel of Philadelphia. The poster solicits agents to sell the book and emphasizes the threat that Mormonism presents to American women. The dedication of the book repeats the concern: "To the Ladies of America whose Sympathies are ever active in behalf of the suffering and oppressed.... In the hope that it will interest them in the condition of their Sisters in moral bondage in Utah."

78. THE STILL ALARM – "DAD'S ON FIRE."
Lithographer: Central Lithographing and
Engraving Co., New York, 1888. 26¼ x 18½.

Across the street from R. H. Macy's store on 14th Street and Sixth Avenue was the popular 14th Street Theatre. Broad comedy was the specialty of the house, which opened its 1887–88 season with the exciting melodrama *The Still Alarm*, by Joseph Arthur. The play was a hit from the beginning, and following its debut in the fall of the year, it returned to the same theatre in the spring of 1888, and ran for more than a hundred additional nights.

The author and Harry Lacy, leading actor in the role of Jack Manley, were proprietors and managers of the show, and the "beautiful twin Arabian horses" that pulled a real fire engine on stage in the second scene of the third act were trained by Lacy. The scene pictured, "Dad's on Fire," appears to be from an earlier scene of the drama.

Joseph Arthur later wrote the even more successful melodrama *Blue Jeans*, which opened at the same theatre in 1890.

79. DANIEL ROCHAT.
Lithographer: Hatch Lithographic Co.,
New York, 1880. 28 x 20⅞.

Scenes from Sardou's drama *Daniel Rochat* in its first New York showing are pictured on the handsome poster from the company of Warner D. Hatch on Vesey Street. A controversial play about the courtship, marriage and eventual divorce of a freethinker and a deeply religious woman, the drama was made pleasing to the public by the "magnificent acting of Palmer's Company and beautiful presentation of the play.... Perhaps Daniel Rochat was the most artistic offering of Palmer's management of Union Square." The theatre annalist George Odell further remarks of this manager in 1880 that "the glorious reign of A. M. Palmer at Union Square Theatre was drawing to a close." Palmer planned to move farther uptown, following the gradual northward displacement of the theatrical center of the city.

The long run that this poster commemorates began on October 16 and lasted until December 15, 1880. The stars were Charles R. Thorne, Jr. as Rochat and Sara Jewett as Lea Henderson.

Victorien Sardou, prolific French creator of "well-made" plays, is best remembered today for pieces, such as *La Tosca*, that he wrote for Sarah Bernhardt.

80. LOTTA; GRAND OPERA HOUSE.
Lithographer: Forbes Co., Boston, 1882.
26½ x 18⅞.

In 1882 at the Grand Opera House, "king of the combination houses of popular appeal . . . Lotta was the bright lure on December 4 in Zip," chronicles George Odell, historian of the New York stage. Three days later, despite the poster notice of Saturday-only matinees, Lotta took part in a midweek matinee performance, a benefit for New York Lodge No. 1 of the Benevolent and Protective Order of Elks. The following week she appeared in a comic pastiche called *Musette*, and then played *The Little Detective* through Christmas Day.

Lotta was Charlotte Crabtree, although the diminutive of her given name was her most frequent stage designation. All charm and breezy Western style, her acting capabilities were almost nonexistent. She was described in her first New York appearance (1864) as having "the face of a beautiful doll and the ways of a kitten." Even the titles of some of her early roles, *Pet of the Petticoats* and *Little Nell*, indicate her blithe and sprightly manner. In this poster she is seen some eighteen years after, still putting on an antic caprice. Small wonder that there is a slightly mad gleam in her eye as this no-longer-juvenile wonder cavorts on her hammock, an Alice-grown-old.

One of the most popular performers of her day, Lotta probably was the greatest money earner on the nineteenth-century American stage. She lived well into the twentieth century as a Boston property owner, and the contesting of her will became a *cause célèbre*.

81. KERRY GOW; O'HARA AND HIS NORA.
Lithographer: Strobridge Lithographing Co.,
Cincinnati, 1882. 26⅞ x 17.

In the spring of 1882 a one-week performance of the Irish drama *Kerry Gow* held the boards of the Grand Opera House at Eighth Avenue and 23rd Street, at the time the farthest

NOTES TO THE PLATES 111

west of any theatre in Manhattan. When it opened in 1869, it was hoped that the house's proximity to the fashionable Chelsea area would bring patrons to its offerings of grand opera, but in the hundred years of its existence every kind of entertainment was offered in this Beaux Arts building with an airy enclosed promenade arcade on the first floor. Its long survival was partially due to multiple use; for a time its upper floors were headquarters for the Erie Railroad.

In the period in which *Kerry Gow* was shown at the Grand Opera House, stars brought in their own companies. In this case, the leading actors were Joseph Murphy as Dan O'Hara and Helen Tracy as Nora Drew. The bold fan-sunburst-and-pinwheel border surrounding a scene from the play is characteristic of many Strobridge posters in this period.

82. *SIBERIA.*
Lithographer: Strobridge Lithographing Co.,
Cincinnati & New York, 1883. 28⅞ x 18¼.

With no real sacrifice of the beautiful border—typical of many on Strobridge theatrical posters of the 1880s—the date and place for the New York opening of Bartley Campbell's *Siberia* is laid-over type. Campbell, whose star began to rise in the early 1870s, was one of the first financially successful native-born American playwrights.

At the time of this play, assassinations in Russia by radical groups were often in the news. In this advertisement one of the play's "sequence of horrors" is illustrated. The dramatic moment pictured here took place on the stage of Haverly's 14th Street Theatre in 1883. The drama had a five-week run with a cast that included Georgia Cayvan as Sara, her movement typified by a critic of the day as "vague and wandering," a description quite unlike the action pictured here.

83. *W. M. DAVENE'S ALLIED ATTRACTIONS; CAPITOLA FORREST.*
Artist: E. Roe (Emil Rothengatter). Lithographer: Strobridge Lithographing Co.,
Cincinnati & New York, 1883. 26½ x 16⅞.

Variety shows took over a number of New York theatres in the 1880s and W. M. Davene was one of the impresarios who brought together a number of these vaudeville turns into theatrical performances, with the thread of a revue to stitch the acts together. Capitola Forrest, vocalist aad skipping-rope dancer, is pictured in an open landscape, where a statue of a satyr lurks behind a tree. Her abbreviated costume—revealing limbs and garter—would have been scandalous for street wear, but was a clear necessity for her jump-rope specialty. Among Davene's other "Allied Attractions" in this decade were Billy Lyons, the female impersonator; six Swiss lady bell ringers; and a farce, *Casey, the Piper.*

84. *CURRIER & IVES ILLUMINATED PICTORIAL POSTERS.*
Artist: Louis Maurer. Lithographers: Currier & Ives, New York, 1890. 27½ x 28½.

The four harness racers dashing before the judging committee in its cozy stand with a cupola on top make a fine advertisement for the illuminated posters of Currier & Ives. The size of the art work offered for sale (not of this poster) is printed below the title. Although the picture is stamped as a specimen copy in three locations, it still exhibits the reason for the great popularity of the firm's prints and posters.

Louis Maurer, the artist, was born in Germany in 1832; he lived to a ripe old age and was still drawing pictures in New York just before his ninety-ninth birthday in 1931. In the early 1850s Maurer was an artist in the firm of N. Currier, specializing in horses, firemen and caricatures. In 1872, he formed a partnership with F. Heppenheimer after having worked with the Major & Knapp Company in the 1860s. In the 1870s he did a series of Butterick fashion plates as part of the commercial work that was almost the entire production of Heppenheimer & Maurer.

85. *CHISEL & STEEL SQUARE WORKS.*
Artist: Charles R. Parsons. Lithographer: Endicott & Co., New York, about 1890.
28½ x 37¾.

This handsome poster offers a number of detailed drawings to inform purchasers of the production and sale of the tools advertised. The views range from a pastoral portrait of the Chisel & Steel Square Works in the hills of southern Vermont to the elegant cast-iron building on Beekman Street in New York City where the tools were sold. On the right, just above the bottom vignette, is an interior view of the New York distributor's shop, the walls lined with cases in which the squares and chisels are displayed in beautiful arrangements that emphasize form repeated in a variety of sizes. At center top the means for transporting the company's goods from the Vermont hills to Manhattan's canyons may be seen in a train stopped at a railroad siding. Steps in the manufacture of the tools are illustrated in the remaining views; at the lower left an overseer is seen in conversation with an owner or potential customer. The artist Parsons (see note to page 22) worked from a building on Beekman Street, one block away from the Thomas Douglass store.

86. *JESSE JAMES COMBINATION.*
Probably New York, 1883. 21¼ x 12½.

The custom of reserving space at the bottom of posters for a flamboyant banner persists through American advertising history. In this dashing puff for the 'Jesse James Combination," the lithographer's name has been obscured in the interests of serving notice of time and place.

Jesse James met his fate in St. Joseph, Missouri, while living under the alias Thomas Howard. On April 3, 1882, two members of his own gang, Charles and Robert Ford, shot him for a $10,000 reward and were commemorated in a popular ballad as "the dirty little coward who shot Mr. Howard." The annalist of the New York theatre, George C. D. Odell, records his amazement at "the epidemic of Jesse James so soon after his death."

James H. Wallack thrilled audiences in his portrayal of the Bandit King at the Windsor Theatre, "the largest playhouse in the city," early in 1883, a year after James's demise. Wallack returned to the Windsor early in the fall season in the same vehicle. Later that year, on November 29, after an evening performance, a fire broke out in the lobby, and the Windsor was destroyed in one of the major theatre fires of the nineteenth century.

87. *PROF D. M. BRISTOL'S EQUESCURRICULUM.*
Lithographer: Courier Lith. Co., Buffalo,
1888. 26½ x 19.

The Courier Co. of Buffalo specialized in circus posters and included Forepaugh's Circus and Wild West Companies among its customers, as well as D. M. Bristol's performing horses. Twenty-two years before the date (1888) penciled on this poster, Professor Bristol appeared at the Third Avenue Theatre in Manhattan, opening the fall season in 1866 and holding that stage for two weeks with the performances of

112 NOTES TO THE PLATES

his trained horses in "Bristol's Equine Wonders." Here, as the professor puts his team through their "Equescurriculum," each horse seems as eager to pose on the staircase as any Follies starlet, while the named team members, Johnnie Sanbourn and Potoskie, demonstrate unequine feats matched only by the unnamed horse's aptitude for multiplication.

88. PECK'S BAD BOY.
Lithographer: Springer Lithographic Co., New York, about 1884. 26 x 11.

The bad boy of the title stands out like a young and mischievous Buddha in this advertisement for the Atkinson Comedy Company of New York. The first performance of the play took place in 1884 at Haverly's Comedy Theatre, with William Carroll in the title role and J. W. Grath as the corner grocery man, one of the boy's chief victims.

The play was based on the then recent humorous stories by George W. Peck (still in print with Dover); Peck's bad boy is a well-known concept in American culture even today. The dramatization remained popular for a long period; as a boy, George M. Cohan played the lead part.

89. MESTAYER-VAUGHN CO.; THE AUTHOR'S HEAD.
Lithographer: Central Lithographing and Engraving Co., New York, about 1885. 26 x 18¼.

The Author's Head was probably presented in the mid-1880s, when its stars, singing entertainers W. A. Mestayer and Theresa Vaughn, were at the height of their career as a comedy team. Other seasons the pair had appeared in such noble dramas as *Tourists in a Pullman Car; Madam Piper; We, Us, and Co.;* and *Wanted a Partner* (a burlesque on an actor's life, also called *Hix's Fix*).

Chained like a fighting pit bull, with flying creatures hovering over his gin-rummied nose, hatchet aimed at temple from within his head, and wall telephone threaded to his ear, the author's head is crowded with subplots ample enough for an epic. The nineteenth-century devotion to phrenology is suggested by the figure's compartmented brain. Undoubtedly the starring actors and their company had a romp with the melodramatic acts pictured within *The Author's Head.*

90. H. L. ETTMAN & CO., IMPORTERS OF SPONGES AND CHAMOIS.
St. Louis, 1897. 20⅞ x 27.

This late nineteenth-century romp illustrates the perils and process of sponge fishing. An androgynous aquatic ballet cavorts in West Indian waters. Many of the fishing boats, though of distinctive and exotic form, yet bear American flags and names, such as *Lester, Lone Star* and *W. J. H. Taylor.*

Drama appears at left and right as a man attempting to get into a vessel "lost his senses and fell back and was drowned"; the net bag for sponges apparently was a contributing factor to his demise. On the right is "A man destroyed by a shark," while the bearded *putto* next to him is, despite his seeming languor, "trying to get away from shark."

In the 1890s Henry L. Ettman and William Sutter of St. Louis imported sponges and copyrighted this delightful poster; one can only ponder where a hunt for the chamois might have taken these intrepid partners.

91. GEO. H. ADAMS' NEW HUMPTY DUMPTY TROUPE.
Artist: E. Roe (Emil Rothengatter). Lithographer: Strobridge Lithographing Co., Cincinnati, possibly 1890. 19⅛ x 27.

This fetchingly mad picnic at the edge of a wood and handy to a stream is possibly from *Humpty Dumpty on a Farm,* presented between Christmas and New Year's in 1890 at the Eighth Street Theatre. The clown and principal actor of the company, George H. Adams, is seen, lower left, holding a bull firmly by its tail.

Adam Forepaugh, circus entrepreneur and animal trainer, was manager of the New Humpty Dumpty Troupe. The name originated in the pantomime play *Humpty Dumpty,* which began a run at the Academy of Fine Arts on March 10, 1863, and continued for 483 performances, breaking the long-run record previously held by *The Black Crook.*

George H. Adams was connected with the New Humpty Dumpty Troupe in the 1880s; in the 1890s another famous clown, Harry Ricketts, was the leading player in a Humpty Dumpty Pantomime Troupe that opened at the Manhattan Opera House in Brooklyn at Christmastime in 1893. The *commedia dell'arte* characters seen here are especially interesting. The comic old man (Pantaloon), Harlequin and Columbine offer stiff competition for the viewer's attention as stilt walkers, puppeteers, acrobats, accordionist and musical-glass expert exhibit their skills.

92. WALTER PELHAM'S ENTERTAINMENT.
Lithographer: E. B. Child, New York, 1892. 20¼ x 12.

One of the twenty characters portrayed in the "original & refined" entertainments offered by Walter Pelham in his evening of "mirth, music, mimicry" is illustrated within the elaborate border: the humorous lecturer Artemus Ward (Charles Farrar Browne), who died in England in 1867. On Washington's Birthday, 1892, Pelham's company appeared in the Y.M.C.A. Hall on 125th Street.

The type used for the main messages on the poster is an unusual and attractive face resembling folded ribbon.

93. PETTS & STRAFFIN'S MINSTRELS.
Lithographer: W. J. Morgan & Co., Cleveland, about 1885. 25⅝ x 19.

This sprightly black-and-white poster, from the large Cleveland firm of W. J. Morgan & Co., illustrates the kinds of acts that enlivened minstrel performances throughout the country. The Petts & Straffin troupe specialized in burlesques of opera and operetta, and examples of these spoofs are painted on the extraordinary drop curtain and in a vignette at the lower right. The scene on the drop curtain is based closely on a Philadelphia poster cut (Public Ledger Job Printing Office) prepared between 1867 and 1875 to advertise Offenbach's operetta *The Grand Duchess of Gerolstein* (included in a selection of such cuts to be published by Dover).

At least two members of the Petts & Straffin troupe assayed both men's and women's roles. A loose-limbed male dancer (lower left) appears in a frilly bonnet (see also upper right), and the clown (top and upper left) is the same person as the dancing doll (lower left). The stage is made to appear splendid and deep by wings and flats painted in Piranesi-like splendor and set forward of a vaguely Egyptian backdrop. The Eastlake design of the proscenium arch echoes theatre design of the period.

NOTES TO THE PLATES 113

*94. THE MOST DELIGHTFUL ROUTE
TO THE SEA SHORE.
Artists: Schell & Hogan. Lithographer:
Charles H. Hart, New York, about 1885.
25⅝ x 19⅜.*

Summer pleasures available to New York residents at the Atlantic shore are suggested in this attractive poster. Open-sided excursion cars were hauled by steam engine from Fort Hamilton through Bath Beach and "Locust Grove" (later Ulmer Park), where a spur line of the Brooklyn, Bath and Coney Island Railroad ended on what was then the longest promenade pier in America. The center illustration looks out to the train terminal and steamboat landing from the open-air ground floor of the Locust Grove Pavilion; Gravesend Bay is beyond. Sighting along the shore from the hotel (lower right), flags mark the Utrecht Club and Marine and Field Club, with Fort Hamilton seen as the dark dot to the left of the sailboat. The view just west from the tip of Coney Island back to the Locust Grove Hotel and Pavilion is shown between the sloop and side-wheeler at the top of the poster.

The Schell and Hogan who drew this delightful Brooklyn scene are unidentified. Schell may be Theodore C. Schell, listed as a painter in the 1885 directory, where six Hogans are listed as painters.

By the end of the century the steam-train ride through the salt marshes had been replaced by trolleys of the Brooklyn Rapid Transit System with "Brilliantly Illuminated and Handsomely Decorated Trolley Excursion Cars for Trolley Parties, Church Picnics, Clubs, Societies, and other outing events." Car rental was ten dollars in the morning, and fifteen and twenty dollars for afternoon and evening "Summer Delights."

*95. THE NEW YORK TIMES.
Artist: "E.P. / 95" [Edward Penfield?].
Lithographers: Liebler & Maass, New York,
1896. 30 x 17.*

This beautiful poster, advertising the Sunday *Times* for February 9, 1896, forecasts the dramatic change that took place in advertising poster design in the last years of the nineteenth century. Graphic designers skillfully transferred the ideas of the Art Nouveau movement to prints and lithograph design, and the art poster became a common means for dispensing advertising information.

This design is one of a series commissioned by *The New York Times* featuring a small tile design in the background. In this period Liebler & Maass, the lithographers, had locations at 224 Centre Street and 1434 Broadway.

The stories advertised are an intriguing introduction to this issue of the *Times:* "Queer National Figures" contains pencil and woodcut sketches of the "Peculiarities of Certain Senators," among whom "Peffer of Kansas was, of course, the First Subject to Attract the Artistic Eye." The lead paragraphs of the story on colonial New York City deal with the Manhattan reaction to a mammoth's tooth found in Claverack in 1705 and to the slave uprising of 1712. Subtitles to the "Haunts of Aaron Burr" blazon forth the news, "New-York City was the Home of his Most Active Years / His Several Habitations Here / The Beautiful Richmond Hill Estate — His Marriage to Mme. Jumel and Its Unhappy consequences," subjects now being explored for the projected publication of the Burr Papers by The New-York Historical Society.

114 NOTES TO THE PLATES

Index of Artists, Engravers, Lithographers, Printers and Publishers

The numbers refer to the pages on which the posters are illustrated; the Notes to the Plates are keyed to the same numbers.

Ackerman, James (379 Broadway, N.Y.C.): 7.
Adrian, W. (Pittsburgh): 69.
American Graphic Co. (N.Y.C.): 30.
American Lithographic Co. (37 City Hall Place, N.Y.C.): 27.
American Oleographic Co. (Milwaukee): 64.
Atwater, Lyman W. (N.Y.C.): 22.

Bencke, H. (N.Y.C.): 36.
Benecke, Thomas (N.Y.C.): 45.
Bensell, C. B. (Philadelphia): 77.
Blanc, A. (Philadelphia): 67.
Brown, Eliphalet, Jr. (142 Fulton St., N.Y.C.): 6, 7.

Calvert Lithographing and Engraving Co. (Detroit): 14, 26.
Calvi, Peter (N.Y.C.): *frontispiece;* 74.
Central Lithographing and Engraving Co. (N.Y.C.): 78, 89.
Child, E. B. (N.Y.C.): 92.
Clay, Cosack & Co. (Buffalo): 23; *see also* Cosack & Co.
Cosack & Co. (Buffalo & Chicago): 66; *see also* Clay, Cosack & Co.
Courier Lith. Co. (Buffalo): 55 right, 87.
Currier, Nathaniel: *see* Currier & Ives.
Currier & Ives (115 Nassau St., N.Y.C.): 22, 84.

Dailey, W. J. (New Cut, Lambeth, London?): 9.
Dalziel, J. (Philadelphia): 77.
Devereux & Brown (N.Y.C.?): 42.
Donaldson Bros. (Five Points, N.Y.C.): 28, 73.

Endicott (George) & Co. (57 Beekman St., N.Y.C.): 21, 48, 85.
E. P.: *see* Penfield, Edward.

Fairmans' Job Printing Office (Elmira, N.Y.): 42.
Forbes, Elisha (Albany): 52.
Forbes Lithography Manufacturing Co. (181 Devonshire St., Boston): 29, 80.
Forst, Averell & Co. (23 Platt St. & 20 Gold St., N.Y.C.): 16.

Gies (Charles) & Co. (Buffalo): 37.
Giffing, W. H. (13 Spruce St., N.Y.C.): 62 left.
Grozelier, Leopold (349 Broadway): 41.

Hart, Charles H. (99 Fulton St., N.Y.C.): 10, 13, 15, 50, 53, 57, 60, 94.
Hatch (Warner D.) & Co., later Hatch Lithographic Co. (29 William St., later 32 Vesey St., N.Y.C.): 13, 18, 79.
Herald Job Print (Fulton & Nassau Sts., N.Y.C.): 46.
Hill, John William (West Nyack, N.Y.): 70.
Hogan (N.Y.C.): 94.
Hopcraft & Co. (21 Barclay St., N.Y.C.): 71.
Howland, W. (N.Y.C.): 63.

Ives, James Merritt: *see* Currier & Ives.

Jones (N.Y.C.): 30.
Juehne, Charles (Albany?): 72.

Knapp, Joseph F. (449 Broadway, N.Y.C.): 11; *see also* Major & Knapp.
Knapp (Joseph P.) Co. (Broadway, & 56 Park Place, N.Y.C.): 38; *see also* Major & Knapp.
Kurz & Allison (Chicago): 35.

Laing, Joseph, & Co. (66 Fulton St., N.Y.C.): 8.
Lewis, G. W. (111 Nassau St., N.Y.C.): 6.
Liebler (Theodore A., Jr.) & (John A. J.) Maass (224 Centre St. & 1434 Broadway, N.Y.C.): 95.

Major, Richard (117 Fulton St., later 449 Broadway, N.Y.C.): 11, 12, 59; *see also* Major & Knapp.
Major & Knapp Engraving, Manufacturing & Lithographing Co. (71 Broadway; 56 Park Place, N.Y.C.): *frontispiece;* 59; *see also* Knapp (Joseph P.) Co.
Maurer, Louis (N.Y.C.): 84.
Merrihew & Son (135 N. 3rd St., Philadelphia): 62 right.
Miller, J.: 67.
Morgan, W. J. & Co. (Cleveland): 93.
Morrell Show Print (511 Arch St., Philadelphia): 55 right.

Nagel (Louis) & (Adam) Weingärtner (74 Fulton St., later 143 Fulton St., N.Y.C.): 41, 45.
National Publishing Co. (Philadelphia & elsewhere): 77.
New York Mercury (22 Spruce St., N.Y.C.): 47.
New-York Scientific American (126 Fulton St., N.Y.C.): 2.
Nugent & Steves (195 Fulton St., N.Y.C.): 76.

Parsons, Charles R. (Beekman St., N.Y.C.): 22, 85.
Pease, Richard H. (Broadway, Albany): 52.
Penfield, Edward (?; N.Y.C.): 95.

Reilley, James (12 Spruce St., N.Y.C.): 55 left.
Roe, E.: *see* Rothengatter, Emil.
Rothengatter, Emil (Cincinnati): 31, 83, 91.

Sackett, Wilhelms & Betzig (45 Rose St., N.Y.C.): 34.
Sarony, Napoleon (117 Fulton St., later 449 Broadway, N.Y.C.): 11, 12.
Sarony & Major, Sarony, Major & Knapp: *see* Sarony, Napoleon; Major, Richard; *and* Knapp, Joseph F.
Schell (Theodore C.?; N.Y.C.): 94.
Schierholz, L. (Hartford): 51.
Schlegel, George (97 William St., N.Y.C.): 68.
Schumacher & (Louis) Ettlinger (13 Murray St., N.Y.C.): 20.
Scientific American: *see* New-York Scientific American.
Scranton, W. (N.Y.C.): 67.
Sebald, H. (Philadelphia?): 77.
Severin, Charles (142 Fulton St., N.Y.C.): 6.
Shearman, James A. (99 Fulton St., N.Y.C.): *frontispiece;* 10, 13, 50, 53, 74.
Shearman & Hart: *see* Shearman, James A., *and* Hart, Charles H.
Shugg, Richard (N.Y.C.?): 47.
Smith, Rae (120 Nassau St., N.Y.C.): 58.
Smith Bros. (N.Y.C.): 70.
Springer Lithographic Co. (N.Y.C.): 88.
Strobridge Lithographing Co. (Cincinnati, N.Y. & London): *inside front cover;* 24, 25, 31, 40, 81, 82, 83, 91.

T. B.: *see* Benecke, Thomas.
Teubner, George W. (N.Y.C.): 3.

Weed (Thurlow), (J. D.) Parsons & Co. (Columbia St., Albany): 72.

Index of Advertisers

The numbers refer to the pages on which the posters are illustrated; the Notes to the Plates are keyed to the same numbers.

Abendroth Bros. (cooking ranges; 109 Beekman St., N.Y.C.): 20.
Adams', George H., New Humpty Dumpty Troupe: 91.
Allen, Mrs. S. A. (hair restorer; 355 Broome St., N.Y.C.?): 11.
American Oleographic Co. (lithographers; Milwaukee): 64.
Atkinson Comedy Co. (N.Y.C.): 88.

Barnes, Stephen D., & Co. (oysters; East St., N.Y.C.): 65.
Barnum's American Museum (Ann St. & Broadway, N.Y.C.): 6, 46 right.
Black Crook, The (stage show): 25.
Boyd, William (confectioner; 383 Broadway, N.Y.C.): 3.
Brewster, J. B., & Co. (carriages); 145 E. 25th St., N.Y.C.): 21.
Bristol's, Prof. D. M., Equescurriculum: 87.
Brunswick, J. M., & Balke Co. (billiard tables; Cincinnati & elsewhere): 35.
Buislay Family (aerialists): 15.
Butterick, E., & Co. (clothing patterns; 555 Broadway, N.Y.C.): 18.

Cable Screw Wire Boots & Shoes (N.Y.C.): 74.
Chisel & Steel Square Works (tools; Shaftsbury, Vt.): 85.
Cincinnati, Hamilton & Dayton R.R. (Cincinnati); *inside front cover.*
Cincinnati Times-Star: *inside front cover.*
Clays, H. (clothing; 8 John St., N.Y.C.): 56.
Coats, J. & P. (thread; Pawtucket & elsewhere): *inside back cover.*
Colt's Patent Fire Arms (Hartford): 51.
Columbia Bicycles: *see* Pope Manufacturing Co.
Congress Stove Polish: 10.
Conklin, E. E., & Co. (ice tools; Rockland Lake, N.Y.): 70.
Cook Carriage Co. (Cincinnati): *inside front cover.*
Crescent Brewing Co. (Aurora, Ind.): *inside front cover.*
Crosby, Butterfield & Haven (shoe machinery; 22 Dey St., N.Y.C.): 58.
Currier & Ives (graphics; 115 Nassau St., N.Y.C.): 84.
Curtis, M. B. (actor): 24.

Daniel Rochat (play): *see* Union Square Theatre.
Davene's, W. H., Allied [Theatrical] Attractions: 83.

Davis', Charles L., Comedy Co.: 31.
Domestic Sewing Machine Co. (14th St. & Broadway, N.Y.C.): 19.
Douglass, Thomas (83 Beekman St., N.Y.C.): *see* Chisel & Steel Square Works.

Electric Extractor Co. (stain remover; Broadway & Fulton St., N.Y.C.): 57.
Estey Organ Co. (Brattleboro): 39.
Ettman, H. L., & Co. (sponges; 11 N. 7th St., St. Louis): 90.
Evans, Edward (clothing; 66 Fulton St., N.Y.C.): 8.

Ferry, D. M., & Co. (seeds; Detroit): 26, 27.
Firth, Hall & Pond (pianos & music; 1 Franklin Square, N.Y.C.): 1.
Foster-Hilson Co. (cigars; 667 First Ave., N.Y.C.): 38.

Gilmore's Garden (theatre; Broadway & Prince St., N.Y.C.): 62 left.
Great Atlantic & Pacific Tea Co. (191 Fulton St., N.Y.C.): 32–33.
Great Western Railway, Great Central Route: 23.
Griffin & Christy's Minstrels (2 W. 24th St., N.Y.C.): 46 left.

Halstead & Co. (meat packers; 194 Forsyth St., N.Y.C.): 36.
Hart, George (roofer; 54 Roosevelt St., N.Y.C.): 53.
Hawes & Graham (wood; 176 Centre St., N.Y.C.): 41.
Hill Bros. (millinery; 564 Broadway, N.Y.C.): 34.
Hinrichs, C. F. A. (toys; 29 Park Place, N.Y.C.): 63.
Hoe, R., & Co. (printing presses; 29 Gold St., N.Y.C.): 16.

Indian Compound (patent medicine): 60.

Jesse James [Theatrical] Combination: 86.
Jollie, Samuel C., & Co. (music & instruments; 385 Broadway, N.Y.C.): 3.

Kanadesaga Nurseries (Geneva, N.Y.): 67.
Kelley, Dr. John Wesley (nostrums; 259 Bowery, N.Y.C.): 44.
Kerry Gow (stage play): 81.

Laing, Joseph, & Co. (lithographers; 66 Fulton St., N.Y.C.): 8.

Locust Grove (seaside resort; Brooklyn, N.Y.): 94.
Lotta (actress): 80.

Manhattan Beach (Brooklyn, N.Y.): 30.
Mestayer-Vaughn [Theatrical] Co.: 89.
Metropolitan Concert Hall (Broadway & 41st St., N.Y.C.): 71.
Miller's, Henry, Tobacco (116 Maiden Lane, N.Y.C.): 12.
Moffat, Dr. William B. (patent medicines; 335 Broadway, N.Y.C.): 43.
Mosler Safe Co. (Hamilton, Ohio): *inside front cover.*
Mulford, Cary & Conklin (leather; 34 Spruce St.. N.Y.C.): 22.
Myers Bros. & Co. (tobacco); Richmond, Va.): 14.

National Publishing Co. (Philadelphia & elsewhere): 77.
New-York Historical Society (E. 11th St. & Second Ave., N.Y.C.): 54.
New York Mercury (magazine; 22 Spruce St., N.Y.C.): 47.
New-York Scientific American (magazine; 126 Fulton St., N.Y.C.): 2.
New York Times (N.Y.C.): 95.

O'Brien, John (circus): 55 left.
Oriental Powder Mills (Cincinnati): *inside front cover.*

Paine, Milton K. (druggist; Windsor, Vt.): 61.
Payn, Benjamin (tobacco; Maiden Lane, Albany) :72.
Payn & McNaughton (tobacco; 7 Broadway, Albany): 4.
Peabody, G. W. (clothing; John & Wall Sts., Kingston, N.Y.): 76.
Peebles, Joseph R., Sons Co. (whisky & cigars; Cincinnati): *inside front cover.*
Pelham's, Walter, Entertainment: 92.
Petts & Straffin's Minstrels: 93.
Pope Manufacturing Co. (bicycles; 597 Washington St., Boston): 28, 29.
Primrose & West (minstrels): 40.

Quick, G. C., & Co. (menagerie): 7.

Ralph & Co. (farm equipment; 23 Fulton St., N.Y.C.): 52.
Rathbun, Benjamin (carriages; Buffalo): 48.
Remington Agricultural Co. (machinery; Ilion, N.Y.): 37.

117

Remington Armory & Sewing Machine Works (Ilion, N.Y.): 75.
Resolute Fire Insurance Co. of the City of N.Y.: 13.
Rice, Jerome B. (seeds; Cambridge, N.Y.): 66.
Richardson, E. B., & Co.: see Kanadesaga Nurseries.
Ridley, Edward, & Sons (millinery; 309 Grand St., N.Y.C.): 68.

Scientific American: see New-York Scientific American.
Shearman & Hart (lithographers; 99 Fulton St., N.Y.C.): 50.

Siberia (stage play): 82.
Silver Tip Shoes: *frontispiece*.
Still Alarm, The (stage play): 78.
St. Nicholas (steamboat; Albany?): 5.

Terry, J. R. (hats & furs; 409 Broadway, N.Y.C.): 59.
Thompson's Life Preserving Seat (N.Y.C.): 45.
Tilton, J. C. (washing machines; Pittsburgh): 69.
Tuttle, George W. (baby exercisers; 311 Broadway, N.Y.C.): 9.
Tyler Batting & Warp Manufacturing Co. (74 Franklin St., N.Y.C.): 73.

Union Square Theatre (N.Y.C.): 79.

Wason [R.R.] Car Manufacturing Co. (Springfield, Mass.): 17.
Westchester Stove Works (69 Warren St., N.Y.C.): 49.
Westovers' Amboy [R.R.] Line: 42.
Whittingham, Anna, J. & E. (millinery; Broadway, N.Y.C.): 3.
Wild West & Great Forepaugh Shows (circus): 55 right.
Wood's Museum (theatre; 1221 Broadway, N.Y.C.): 62 right.

Chronological Index of Posters

The numbers refer to the pages on which the posters are illustrated; the Notes to the Plates are keyed to the same numbers.

1842 (about): 1.
1845 (about): 2, 3.
1847 (about): 4.
1849: 5.
1850: 7.
1850 (about): 9, 41.
1851–52: 6.
1852: 44.
1853: 42.
1854: 45.
1854 (about): 8.
1855 (about): 12, 52.
1856: 46 right.
1858: 49.
1859: 47.
1860 (about): 11, 43, 48.
1861 (about): 10.
1862 (about): 51.

1863 (about): 13, 50.
1864: 54.
1864 (about): 53.
1866: 15, 55 left.
1867: 46 left, 56, 59.
1867 (about): 14.
1868 (about): 58, 65.
1870 (about): 16, 57, 60, 66.
1872: 17, 62 right.
1873: 18, 63, 69.
1874 (about): 19.
1875: 64.
1875 (about): 67, 68, 70, 72, 74, 75.
1876: 20, 21, 23.
1876 (about): 61.
1877: 22, 63.
1880: 79.
1880 (about): *frontispiece;* 26, 71, 76.

1881 (about): 25.
1882: 24, 77, 80, 81.
1883: 82, 83, 86.
1884 (about): 88.
1885: *inside back cover, left;* 30, 31.
1885 (about): 28, 34, 35, 73, 89, 93, 94.
1886: 32–33, 36.
1886 (about): 29.
1888: 55 right, 78, 87.
1890: 84.
1890 (about): *inside back cover, right;* 27, 37, 39, 85, 91.
1892: 62 left, 92.
1893 (about): 38.
1894: *inside front cover;* 40.
1896: 95.
1897: 90.

119